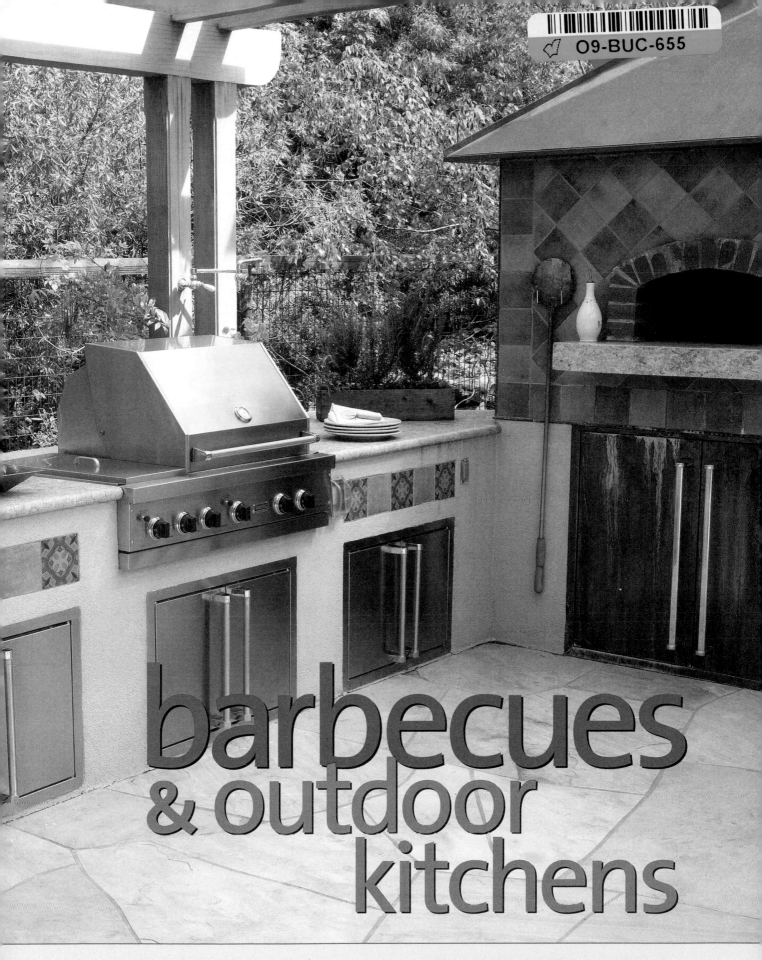

barbecues
& outdoor
kitchens

By Steve Cory and the Editors of Sunset Books 🔥 Menlo Park, California

contents

SUNSET BOOKS

vice president, general manager: Richard A. Smeby

vice president, editorial director: Bob Doyle

production director: Lory Day

operations director: Rosann Sutherland

marketing manager: Linda Barker

art director: Vasken Guiragossian

special sales: Brad Moses

cover: Photography by Frank Gaglione;

      Photo Styling by Laura Del Fava;

      Design by Ransohoff, Blanchfield, Jones, Inc.

10 9 8 7 6 5

First Printing January 2006

For additional copies of *Barbecues & Outdoor
Kitchens* or any other Sunset book, call
1-800-526-5111 or visit us at www.sunset.com.

STAFF FOR THIS BOOK

managing editor: Bridget Biscotti Bradley

writer: Steve Cory

art director: Alice Rogers

copy editor: John Edmonds

illustrator: Ian Worpole

technical consultant: Sergio de Paula

prepress coordinator: Danielle Javier

proofreader: Meagan C. B. Henderson

indexer: Nanette Cardon

production specialist: Linda M. Bouchard

planning your outdoor kitchen

HOMEOWNERS HAVE LONG APPRECIATED the benefits of cooking, dining, and entertaining outdoors. With fresh air and the sounds of nature or the neighborhood, people find life's stresses tend to melt away and the prospect of good food becomes the only concern. Not so long ago, outdoor cooking typically meant a tiny grill, little or no working space, numerous trips to and from the house, and a weathered picnic table that tended to spill the iced tea. Increasingly, however, people are taking steps to claim the outdoors as an extension of the comforts and convenience of home. Manufacturers have responded with an array of products: large-capacity grills that make the cooking easier, pizza ovens, cabinets suitable for outdoors, refrigerators, sinks, overhead protection, even climate-control features. There is something for every budget, and even modest upgrades can improve the experience. This chapter will guide you through all aspects of planning an outdoor kitchen.

Left: *Cheery painted accents brighten this outdoor space and coordinate the cooking area with the porch. The basic counter unit houses a spacious grill with a rotisserie in the rear.* **Below:** *A stately brick cabinet blends seamlessly with the home's exterior. The large grill is equipped with a side burner, and there is enough counter space for preparing main courses as well as side dishes.*

area that could otherwise be used for gardening or play. If you grill only occasionally, an elaborate outdoor kitchen that is mostly idle may stare back at you and inspire buyer's remorse.

starting small

These days, a modest outdoor kitchen consists of a built-in propane or charcoal grill set into a 6-foot-long counter with a couple of cabinets for storage below. If you're used to grilling on a stand-alone unit with a tiny surface for setting a platter or two, a setup like this will be a major upgrade, providing a stable cooking appliance and plenty of counter space for preparing salads and vegetables.

For the simplest installation, purchase a prefab all-in-one unit, which may include a refrigerator but probably not a sink. Some units include overhead structures with lights.

Consider a modest-sized outdoor kitchen if your yard space is at a premium. A large kitchen in a small yard might monopolize an

Build a fire pit out in the yard. This simple installation will add friendly campfirelike experiences to your repertoire and make the outdoor kitchen feel expansive.

■ Add simple amenities. Most of the options shown on pages 31–33 require no plumbing or wiring and can be hung or installed with little effort. Great-looking patio furniture quickly enhances the setting. Low-voltage lighting creates a mellow ambiance for a small outlay of money and time.

Above: This outdoor kitchen includes the most basic element, the grill, gracefully perched atop a counter that segues into a stone wall. There is plenty of space to add other kitchen amenities as time and budget permit. Below: Built into a wall that wraps around a porch, this outdoor kitchen blends into the background, and there's still space for added touches such as a sink and refrigerator.

BUILDING IN STAGES

It's often possible to start small with the idea of adding on later. For instance, build a simple attached counter with a barbecue now and see how often you end up eating outdoors. If you find your appetite has been whetted, you can extend the counter outward and perhaps add a pizza oven or upright barbecue.

ADDED TOUCHES

To take the simple counter with grill a step or two further, consider these options, all of which are pretty easy to install:

■ Add a raised counter or bar, either to the side of or opposite the cooking counter, for dining with stools. This arrangement brings family members and friends closer to the cook, turning barbecuing and dining into a seamless communal experience.

■ If you have a nearby outdoor electrical receptacle, hooking up a refrigerator may be a matter of simply running an outdoor-rated extension cord.

■ Installing an electrical line and a receptacle near the counter will allow you to use electric appliances.

■ If the counter is near the house (especially if it is on the same wall as the kitchen sink), it may be inexpensive to hook up a sink (see pages 144–147).

on a grander scale

A full-blown outdoor kitchen typically contains a host of cooking options—grill with side burner, fireplace, pizza oven, warming drawer, refrigerator—and perhaps amenities such as outdoor lighting and heaters. But a successful kitchen and dining area is more than a collection of appliances. It is carefully designed with two goals in mind: to bring your family and friends together in a beautiful setting, and to make cooking outdoors easy and relaxing.

CHOOSING A STYLE

Consider hiring a designer, as you likely would for an indoor kitchen. Choose a landscape architect or kitchen designer with an appealing portfolio of outdoor kitchens.

Perhaps you would enjoy a Tuscan style, with stuccoed counters and walls painted in a warm

Comfortable and well equipped, this outdoor kitchen has all the trappings of an indoor kitchen, save the walls. Outdoor rooms, in keeping with the scale of the overall landscape, can be larger than indoor spaces but still nicely proportioned.

color, large beams overhead, and stonework. For a homey American look, consider brick counters and columns, tiled countertops, and an overhead made with stained lumber. A sleek, modern style might include countertops made of granite or polished concrete, and counters and columns covered with stucco and painted white or a bright color.

Above: This stunning kitchen, built by the homeowner, features stone facing, a pizza oven, and polished concrete countertops. The drinking fountain at right is made of the same color concrete as the countertops. Right: A narrow side yard is often just the right size for two or more gathering areas. The furniture in the foreground is suited to drinks and snacks, while the far area is arranged for comfortable dining.

Left: *Massive wooden pillars reminiscent of Greek columns support an overhead structure built out from the house's roof, providing stylish protection from the elements. In addition to a grill and cooktop, a niche holds an electric roaster.* **Below:** *A wall with a whimsical window defines the outdoor kitchen space from its vast, high-desert surroundings.*

SPACIOUS YET FRIENDLY

Don't let the size of the kitchen get out of hand; aim for a space that will encourage happy times with family members and friends. Even if the kitchen-dining area has three or four major cooking facilities plus a table that seats 12, it need not be larger than 300 square feet.

Most people like to place the dining area in the center of things. For many families, it works well to have two separate eating areas: a normal-sized table (or eating counter) for family meals and small gatherings, and a larger table for grand parties located a bit farther away.

If the idea of multiple gathering areas appeals to you, consider these possibilities:

- A small coffee table near a fireplace is a great place to enjoy a drink or a game of cards.
- If you are building a pool at the same time as the kitchen, perhaps install a bar pool, which features a wet bar with a counter about a foot above the pool, and in-pool stools, so people can swim up to the bar.
- A small fireplace next to a spa or hot tub creates a wonderful atmosphere.

UNDERGROUND SYSTEMS

While many outdoor kitchens are fairly simple to install, some large-scale projects have a lot going on underground. Ovens and fireplaces require strong concrete footings. Gas and water supply lines may need to run in deep trenches from the house to new appliances and sinks (see pages 108–109). Sinks also need drain lines. In a large installation, these lines may run long distances, so it is usually best to hire professional concrete layers, plumbers, and electricians.

planning and design

To ensure that you'll appreciate your outdoor space for years to come, take your time making design decisions and choosing materials.

Fortunately, masonry surfaces almost always blend well with surrounding foliage, as well as with other outdoor building products—large or small stone, brick, tile, stone tile, concrete, or stucco. Still, choose materials carefully, placing the different elements next to each other to ensure that they will harmonize. Also keep in mind that practical considerations go hand in hand with aesthetics. Some landscaping features are designed primarily for appearance, but an outdoor kitchen must also work.

EXPLORING POSSIBILITIES

Before you tackle the specifics of your design, think about the big picture. Above all, you want to include elements that will make you happy and comfortable in your new outdoor setting. Think about how many people you typically entertain and what sorts of outdoor cooking you most enjoy.

Consider new possibilities as well. Flipping through this book will give you plenty of ideas. For instance, you may take a fancy to a fire pit, a pizza oven, or a churrasco barbecue (see pages 16–19). Or you may be interested in a new type of countertop or an unusual covering for the outside of the counter. If any of these possibilities intrigues you, visit homeowners who have similar outdoor kitchens, or find samples at stone yards and home improvement centers to see whether they will suit your needs.

Pulling all the details together into a unified design that works with the house and landscape can be a fun process. The goal is to make the most of your yard's assets while minimizing any drawbacks.

This cooking area fits so serenely within its rock garden setting that the flowers dotting the landscape are more noticeable than the cooking equipment. The large boulders were specially cut to accommodate both the grill and the pizza oven.

and a light smoky flavor. And the meat cooked in an upright churrasco barbecue structure is unforgettably juicy and tender (see pages 17 and 93–95).

Once you have determined the types of cooking you want to do outdoors, consider the maximum number of people you will cook for on any given occasion. To help guide your design, plan out several sample meals. Make sure that your cooking center can handle the quantity of food and the required preparation, and that your entertaining area can comfortably accommodate your guests.

COOKING STYLES

When most people use the term "barbecuing," they actually mean grilling. Grilling is simply the process of cooking food over high heat on a cooking grate. True barbecuing, a style of cuisine that originated in the southern United States more than a century ago, is often referred to as "smoking": slow-cooking large pieces of meat in a smoke-filled chamber that burns hardwoods. (If this is your style of cooking, see the smoker project on pages 89–92.)

By far the most popular cooking appliance in outdoor kitchens is the built-in (or drop-in) grill. It fits into a counter that has been specially built with an opening just the right size. But there's no rule that says you can't also have a stand-alone unit to add to

your range of cooking styles. See pages 28–30 for a wide variety of appliances that grill, smoke, fry, boil, sauté, and rotisserie.

In addition, having several special amenities and utensils makes it possible to expand your outdoor cooking repertoire well beyond the traditional burgers and hotdogs. See pages 32–33 to peruse the latest gadgets that make it fun and easy to cook fish, vegetables, and meat, to name a few of the possibilities.

Any kind of cooking you enjoy inside your home can now be accomplished outdoors, often with better results. People who choose a wood-fired pizza oven (see pages 16–17), which can crank up the heat to 750 degrees, can produce pizzas and breads with wonderfully crunchy crusts

A gas grill can be used to cook a three-course meal, from grilled vegetable appetizers to meat and potatoes and even grilled fruit for desert. This built-in unit sits in a ceramic tile countertop, which offers plenty of room for preparation.

LOCATION

The first decision you make may be whether to place the kitchen against the house or some distance away in the yard. Either option has advantages and disadvantages.

An outdoor room that is near or attached to the house may borrow overhead protection from the house. Installation is much easier if you can simply run electrical and plumbing lines through a shared wall. And food preparation is simplified when the kitchen is just outside the door. However, be careful that the grill is not so close to the house as to create a fire hazard (see next page). Also make sure that prevailing winds won't blow too much smoke into the house.

A kitchen located away from the house can be an enchanting retreat. However, installing electrical and plumbing lines may be difficult. In particular, it may be impossible to run a sink drain line into the house, so you may need to route it to a dry well or to the city storm drain (see pages 108–109). Also, carting food and dishes from the house will be a lot more difficult.

A successful design can be very simple. This outdoor kitchen is right outside the back door of the house, and includes a warm fireplace and dining table. There is just enough room for traffic to flow easily past the cooks.

SIZE AND SHAPE

Once you have chosen your location, mark off the area with rope or a garden hose to get a feel for the space. Position lawn furniture and posts to mimic counters and other structural elements that you might install. Consult pages 36–39 to start designing a space that will work.

Note how you move around this area and what effect the structures will have. For instance, will the design inhibit your traffic patterns? Will it obstruct the view, either from the outdoor dining table or from an inside window? Can you orient the kitchen so you can keep an eye on the kids while you cook?

Nestled snugly between groupings of palms in a tropical setting, this galley-style kitchen has openings on both ends so people can get from the patio to the seating area beyond.

FIRE SAFETY

Check with your local building department to make sure you will not violate fire codes, and also use common sense. A gas grill produces flames similar to those of an indoor cooktop, and charcoal grills may occasionally throw flames a foot high. Neither represents a grave fire hazard as long as you keep the cooking units several feet from an overhead wood structure or nearby plants. Some grills have sleeves that make them nearly cool to the touch, so they can abut a wood counter.

Fire pits need more space (see pages 86–88). Any source of fire should be off the beaten path so that people, especially children, will not have to get too close.

Charcoal grills can sometimes flare up, so use caution at all times.

HOOKUPS

Many outdoor kitchen appliances require no hookups with the house. These include a charcoal or propane grill, a wood-fired pizza oven or upright barbecue, and a fire pit with no gas nozzle. However, many components do require connections:

- A sink with a faucet needs water supply pipes, a drain line of some sort, and perhaps an under-counter water heater (see pages 144–147).

- If you want to use an electric appliance like a blender or food processor, you will need to run a safe electrical line and install receptacles. A refrigerator also requires an outlet. Bright standard-voltage lights call for serious electrical work, though low-voltage lights are easier to install (see page 143).

- A gas grill can be hooked to a simple propane tank in the counter below, but a gas line from the house will provide a more convenient source of fuel. In most areas, gas is less expensive than propane, but the reverse may be the case in your locale. A gas-fired fire pit or fireplace will also need a line. See page 108 for information about running gas lines.

All of these hookups, except for the low-voltage lights, are serious construction projects. They must be installed safely and be in compliance with local building codes. You will need a permit from your local building department, and you'll probably need to schedule inspections at two or more stages. After reading the relevant sections in this book, you may choose to hire a professional plumber or electrician to run the lines, even if you do the rest of the work yourself.

FLOOR, CEILING, AND WALLS

Most outdoor kitchens rest atop a patio made of bricks, tile, concrete pavers, or a slab of concrete. If you don't have a patio, or if you want to change the one you have, consult Sunset's *Complete Patio Book*, where you will find design tips and step-by-step instructions for laying any type of patio.

Because vertical elements are much more visible than the floor, some homeowners are content to leave a plain-looking patio in place rather than go to the extra expense of building a new one. Concrete decorating companies can beautify an old slab by acid-staining it or by applying a colored and textured polymer coating. Or you can apply tile, flagstone, or brick to the concrete slab later.

Often a new patio is laid at the same time kitchen counters are constructed, but it is usually possible to set the counter on an existing patio. Your patio may be strong enough to support a concrete block counter. Consult your local building department to be sure. But you may need to tear up the patio and pour a thick concrete footing to support the counter, especially if you fill the block cells with concrete (see page 117). If the patio is not strong enough, consider building with wood or steel stud framing instead of block. If you plan to build a massive structure like a fireplace or a pizza oven, you will definitely need to pour a thick concrete footing. If you have a

*Above: The vertical elements in this outdoor room add interest that is intensified by the linear shadows cast by overhead slats. The columns serve as oversized picture windows that frame the sweeping view. **Below:** A small-scale outdoor kitchen was the right choice for this wooden deck, as a larger structure would have been too heavy. The solid roof provides a dry, shady place for an elegant meal.*

deck, a block counter will be too heavy for it. Build with wood or steel studs instead (see pages 122–125). In a very dry climate, you may be able to skip building the substructure and simply install wood cabinets.

Taming the elements—sun, rain, and wind—is necessary for the space to be comfortable. A variety of overhead structures can help with sun and rain. Be sure to plan for one from the start of your project. See pages 20–21 for suggestions on dealing with wind.

DO IT YOURSELF OR HIRE A PRO?

Carefully read through the instructions in this book that apply to the projects you have chosen. Many are within reach of a handy homeowner but require some practice. If you lack experience in certain phases of a project, decide whether you want to learn the skills or hire a pro. In many cases, mistakes can be more costly than contracting out the work from the start.

You will save labor costs by doing the building yourself, but remember to place a value on your time. If in a day or two a professional can build a project that would take you five or six weekends, you may want to reconsider doing the work yourself unless you enjoy the process. Be realistic about how much free time you have. If you can spare only a few hours a week, construction may last an entire summer.

Traditional materials, curved lines, and bright colors create a unique look. An outdoor living space like this generally calls for professional designers and installers.

Outdoor construction generally does not disrupt family life the way an indoor renovation does. This being the case, a summer-long project may be enjoyable. Just make sure the construction will not hinder traffic into the house or become an eyesore that angers your neighbors.

Beware of harming yourself. Masonry work often calls for repeatedly lifting small to medium loads. If you are not used to this sort of work, and especially if you are middle-aged or older, you may feel fine while you are working but wake up the next morning with severe back strain. Pace yourself, stand and stretch from time to time, and perhaps hire help for some of the lifting.

BUDGETING

Develop a budget and stick to it. Carefully list all the expenses. As with indoor kitchens, appliances can easily cost more than labor and materials. A less pricey appliance may not impress the neighbors, but it may work fine for your purposes.

Even if you plan to do most of the work yourself, extra costs beyond materials and appliances tend to crop up. You may incur expenses for permits, deliveries, tools, and perhaps the services of a designer. And you may need to hire a professional for some aspects of the job, such as wiring or plumbing.

A wood-burning pizza oven can heat up to 750 degrees, with delicious results. Generally, a purchased insert is housed in a massive masonry structure that can safely contain that level of heat.

pizza ovens and other cooking options

Here are three exciting ways to cook outdoors for results that are definitely a cut above the ordinary.

Wood-burning ovens made of clay have been around for thousands of years. A wood-fired oven reaches heat unattainable in an indoor oven; 750 degrees is common. In addition, the oven's fire-heated ceramic material radiates heat evenly and intensely. The results include breads with a crunchy crust and meats that are crispy on the outside and tender on the inside.

You may find an artisan in your area who specializes in such ovens. If you hire someone to custom-build one, check with previous customers to make sure their ovens draw well and produce intense, even heat.

PIZZA OVENS

Today, the most common wood-fired oven for outdoor kitchens is a pizza oven. In a typical installation you would purchase the oven insert, then build a massive structure to support and insulate the insert (see pages 76–79). The oven insert may be made of a special Italian clay or of refractory concrete combined with fire-bricks. Both produce pizzas with bubbly-crunchy crusts and a subtle smoky taste. It takes about half an hour to build a wood fire in a pizza oven; the pizza then cooks in two or three minutes.

In a typical setup, firewood for the pizza oven is kept within easy reach in a storage bin just below.

ADOBE OVENS

This low-tech alternative to a pizza oven can become a sculpted work of art. The basic oven is simply an enclosure made of hardened mud, with a door opening in the front and a vent hole in the rear. The quality of the mud is crucial, but with some luck and effort you can find the right mixture (see pages 83–85 for building instructions). Once the oven is built, the outside structure can be made into most any shape, and either painted or left a natural color. The black char mark over the door is considered an indispensable part of the look.

CHURRASCO BARBECUES

A churrasco barbecue is a small fireplace about shoulder high. You build a small fire of wood charcoal (not mineral-filled briquettes) under a rotisserie with spits at two or more heights above the fire.

Sometimes referred to as Brazilian or Gaucho style, churrasco began as a method for rendering tougher, open-range beef more tender. With store-bought cuts, the results are exceptionally tender and juicy.

A churrasco cooks differently than a simple rotisserie over a grill, because it has the added dimension of heat radiating from the ovenlike walls. Even the side of the meat facing away from the

fire is cooked, and the radiant heat helps seal in the juices. In a typical setup, the lower rotisserie spits rotate mechanically, while the upper spits are turned by hand every few minutes. Few juices drip onto the fire below.

Above: Two adobe ovens are molded onto a meandering bench. The whole structure is painted milky white for a dreamy effect. *Below:* This churrasco rotisserie insert can cook large quantities of meat or vegetables at once, making it perfect for backyard barbecue parties. For more information on how to build the colorful unit below, see the project on pages 93–95.

fire pits and fireplaces

Whether encased in a fireplace with a hearth or open to the elements in a pit, an open fire is sure to become a focal point for a relaxing post-dinner evening under the stars.

While kids may clamor to use an open fire for roasting hot dogs or marshmallows, you can use it for serious cooking as well. Fire pits and fireplaces can be equipped with spits, tripods, grates, and rotisseries. Such cooking may be less convenient and a bit sweatier than cooking on a grill or oven, but many people enjoy the primitive nature of the experience.

A fire pit is basically a hole in the ground with a decorative stone or brick ring constructed around it. Building one is a simple masonry project (see pages 86–88). If you want a gas-powered fire,

you will need to run a gas line into the pit. Be sure to place the pit where flames and sparks cannot create a fire hazard.

You can also buy a portable metal fire pit. Simply put it in a safe spot on a nonflammable surface and build a fire.

An outdoor fireplace is built much the same as an indoor one.

You don't have to worry as much about venting, but you do want the flue to draw smoke up the chimney rather than out the firebox. Getting a strong draw is tricky; the firebox and flue must be built just right. Either hire a pro to build a fireplace from scratch, or purchase a kit that you can assemble yourself.

Above: *Adding a large masonry structure such as this upright fireplace can make the overall house design more appealing. The classic lines of this fireplace are the perfect complement to the home's exterior.*
Left: *A cast-concrete fireplace like this can be a wood-burning portable unit or hooked up to a gas line.*

This single structure has two chimneys: one for a pizza oven and one for a large fireplace. The fireplace is angled slightly to subtly create a separate lounging area in front.

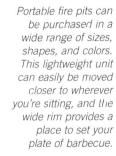

A gas-powered fireplace with ceramic stones is the perfect choice for a retro-style patio and pool. S'mores, anyone?

Portable fire pits can be purchased in a wide range of sizes, shapes, and colors. This lightweight unit can easily be moved closer to wherever you're sitting, and the wide rim provides a place to set your plate of barbecue.

overheads and protection from wind

An overhead structure is an integral part of most outdoor kitchen designs. People often build an outdoor kitchen and then later realize that they need some protection against the elements. Most commonly, shade is needed, but protection against rain can also be an issue. Be sure to run your plans past the local building department to make sure your overhead is not so close to a grill or other heat source as to pose a fire hazard (see page 13).

OVERHEADS

An overhead can often be built later, after the kitchen is finished and you know just where you need shade. However, it is usually easier in the long run to at least set the posts and basic framing while the kitchen is being built. See pages 150–153 for tips on planning for shade and installing an overhead.

In addition to providing protection, an overhead is an important decorative element. It helps define the space, turning it into a genuine room while still allowing plenty of sun through.

WALLS

Strong winds, either occasional or seasonal, can disturb the peace and disrupt dining and cooking. Wind often flows like water, spilling over obstacles, breaking into currents, and swirling around the house.

A vertical structure such as a wall or solid fence is usually not an effective wind barrier. It will

AWNINGS

An awning can provide shelter from both sun and rain. A number of companies specialize in awnings, and many make products that are durable, attractive, and easy to operate. Some open and close with the turn of a crank, while others are motorized. Awning fabric is typically made of several layers of different materials. Look for at least a 5-year warranty against deterioration and color fading. An awning should be kept a safe distance from open flames or cooking appliances.

For maximum protection from the elements, some outdoor kitchens include a shingled roof and two or more walls with large removable windows that can be replaced with screens in summer. Such a kitchen must have adequate ventilation for cooking. Building such a structure calls for standard framing and roofing techniques (see Sunset's *Building Screened Rooms* for more information).

provide effective protection for only a small area—roughly the same distance as the height of the barrier. Farther away, wind will swirl downward onto the patio. A barrier with openings—such as a fence made with lattice or spaced pickets, or a series of shrubs— will diffuse rather than block the wind, and it will provide more even protection for a larger area. Such a barrier is also friendlier to neighbors and usually more attractive than a solid fence.

A fireplace and two overhead infrared space heaters add warmth to the seating areas. Lattice and climbing plants provide ample protection from the wind.

counters

Like their indoor counterparts, outdoor counters usually measure 36 inches from the floor to the surface of the countertop. That's the most comfortable working height for most adults. An eating counter will be higher, commonly 42 inches.

One of the great advantages of a counter is the storage space it offers. For a selection of doors, drawers, and other in-counter storage options, see page 25. Countertops are usually made of different materials than the counters they cover (see pages 26–27 for options).

SUBSTRUCTURE

Most commonly, outdoor counters are built of 6-inch-wide concrete block, also called concrete masonry units or CMUs (see pages 112–117). However, you can also build with wood studs, or steel studs covered with concrete backerboard (see pages 122–125). If you plan to face your counter with brick, you may choose to build a brick structure (see pages 118–121). Counters can also be built of large stones or poured concrete, but those options are more difficult and have no real advantages over block or backerboard.

Stones of various sizes, shapes, and colors have an informal appeal that works in any outdoor setting. They provide a pleasing contrast with the countertop tiles and the stainless-steel accessories.

FINISH MATERIALS

Concrete block or backerboard can be finished with any material that can stand up to the elements. The following two pages detail the most common choices:

NATURAL STONE Thin stones suitable for covering a vertical surface may be called face stone, flagstone, or veneer stone. At a stone yard or brickyard, you will find large pallets of various types of face stone, which you can purchase by weight. A salesperson should be able to help you estimate how much you need to cover your counters. Be aware that some stone, especially granite and limestone, can be very difficult to cut, while other types, such as sandstone, cut easily. See pages 128–129 for installation instructions.

FAUX STONE Often called architectural stone veneer, these are difficult to distinguish from natural stone. However, they are lighter and easier to cut, and they come with specially sized stone pieces for corners. All of this makes them much easier to install than natural stone. For instructions, see page 129.

STONE AND CERAMIC TILES Natural stone can be cut into even, straight-sided squares. Slate tile from India, Africa, and Mexico has an irregular surface texture and comes in a stunning array of colors. Polished granite, travertine, and marble tile have a stately appearance.

Ceramic tiles come in a limitless variety of colors, shapes, and textures. Consult a tile dealer to be sure the tiles will survive in your climate. Mexican saltillos and terra-cotta tiles have a warm, reddish brown glow. Glazed tiles have a durable shiny surface. Porcelain tiles can be manufactured to resemble most any type of ceramic or stone tile. See pages 130–131 for installing stone or ceramic tile on a counter.

Above: Slate tiles cover this impressive counter, which houses a pizza oven on the other side. The different levels add interest and provide shelf space. **Left:** These faux stones are nearly impossible to distinguish from the real thing. Their long rectangular shapes, and the fact that there is no mortar in the joints, give the feel of an old-fashioned garden wall.

BRICK Reassuringly traditional and naturally warm in color, brick blends with many home styles. Common brick, which has touches of white, is a popular choice, but a wide variety of face bricks are available, ranging from dark reddish brown to yellow. Most bricks are rough in texture, but some have a smooth, glazed face. Laying brick requires patience and some skill (see pages 118–121).

STUCCO Usually applied over concrete block or brick, stucco gives a barbecue a finished look, especially next to a stuccoed home. Stucco is applied in two or three coats, each of which requires a day or more to dry, so application is somewhat time consuming. Textures range from very bumpy to nearly smooth (see pages 126–127 for techniques).

*Top: A simple rectangular brick counter is within reach of a do-it-yourselfer. Common brick has a timeless appeal and is fun to dress up with accessories. Here stainless steel, granite, and nearby foliage elevate the overall effect. **Above:** This stucco has a relatively smooth troweled finish.*

WOOD CABINETS

In a warm, dry climate, you may choose to install solid wood kitchen cabinets. Be sure to keep them well coated with sealer or paint, both inside and outside. Another alternative is to build your own cabinets using T1-11 or another exterior siding material.

DOORS, DRAWERS, AND STORAGE OPTIONS

By installing a door in a counter, you gain access to the cavity inside, where you can store cooking implements, charcoal, and perhaps a propane tank. If you have a sink, you will need this space for the plumbing.

Be aware that many built-in barbecue grills do not fully seal around their edges. During heavy rain, water will likely seep into the storage space. Drill holes in the counter's floor for water to run through, and store items on a pallet.

Purchase cabinet doors and drawers from a manufacturer that specializes in outdoor kitchen products. Stainless steel is the most popular choice, but also consider black powder-coated units, which are just as durable yet easier to keep clean.

Getting at the space behind a door usually means crouching or kneeling, especially if you need to reach a small item. Consider installing drawers for small implements.

For even greater convenience, buy a stainless-steel counter unit that already contains drawers and doors of various sizes.

You can even buy an electric oven drawer, also called a warming drawer, to keep food hot while you're cooking multiple batches or other courses. It typically plugs into a standard 120-volt receptacle.

Top: These Euro-style stainless-steel components can be assembled easily. A warming drawer is conveniently located right under the grill. Banks of drawers make it possible to equip this area with all the conveniences of an indoor kitchen.
Above: Metal shelving units are sold in a variety of configurations. Choose one with slide-out trays to store smaller items more efficiently.
Left: This rustic counter features two doors that were salvaged from old furnaces, and one cobbled together out of distressed wood.

countertops

ndoor countertops are typically 24 inches deep, while outdoor countertops are 30 inches or deeper. If the countertop will be accessible from both sides, you may want to make it 42 inches or more.

SUBSTRATE

If the countertop will be made of concrete or thick slabs of stone, it will likely not need support other than the counter's walls. However, most other finish materials will need to rest on a solid subsurface that spans the counter and extends 3 inches or so on either side.

The most common substrate options are a steel-reinforced concrete slab (see pages 136–139), or two thicknesses of concrete backerboard that are glued together with thinset mortar (see page 132).

FINISH MATERIALS

The kitchen's working surfaces, which may also be used as dining surfaces, should be durable and easy to clean. There are several finish materials that will achieve these goals beautifully.

*Above: Almost white natural stone tiles add an elegant touch to a curved countertop. Matching white chair cushions accentuate the clean design. **Right:** A granite slab countertop typically is made with an edging piece under the top piece. Once the pieces are mortared in place, the joint between them is ground and polished until it becomes almost invisible, giving the appearance of a very thick slab.*

STONE TILE Stone tiles of any sort can be used on a countertop as long as they are protected with a coat or two of acrylic sealer. Some stone tiles that do fine on a vertical surface may be unsuitable for countertop duty, either because they are not strong enough or because they stain easily. See pages 22–23 for basic information on stone tiles and pages 130–131 for installation. Consult a tile dealer before making your choice.

GRANITE Large, gleaming slabs of granite make ideal countertops, both indoors and out. Granite is typically speckled or flecked, and it comes in a wide variety of shades ranging from very dark to very light. Cutting and installing a granite slab is best left to

professionals. Usually there is no need for a substrate, since the granite slab is very strong. Installers will measure your counter, cut the slab or slabs at their shop, and set the counter. To achieve the illusion of a very thick slab, they may attach a facing piece, typically 2 inches wide, below the front edge of the slab, then grind and polish the seam until you can barely see it.

GLAZED CERAMIC TILE This is a popular choice for indoor and outdoor counters because glazed tiles are easy to wipe clean. Take a drawing of your countertop to a tile dealer and choose an ensemble that includes field (regular) tiles as well as all the special pieces you will need to cover edges and corners. See pages 132–135 for installation instructions.

STONE SLAB A smooth slab of stone, typically 3 inches thick, can simply be laid on top of the counter. In most cases, you will want to hire a mason or a stone yard to cut the slabs to fit. Popular choices include bluestone and limestone.

DECORATIVE CONCRETE Once thought of as irredeemably dull and gray, concrete now offers exciting decorating possibilities. It can be imbued with color while it is wet or acid-stained after it has cured. A concrete top may have a rough surface, especially at the edges, or it can be ground smooth as polished marble. Many contractors who specialize in concrete counters are artisans who can create a one-of-a-kind top for you. If you have basic masonry skills and are ambitious, you may want to try it yourself. See pages 136–139 for techniques.

BRICK AND FLAGSTONE These may seem unlikely choices for a working surface, since they are not smooth and tend to be porous. However, many types of brick and some flagstones (especially granites and slates) have a hard finish that can be kept clean. An application of acrylic sealer every year or so can make even common brick or rough limestone fairly easy to clean. (Sandstone is simply not a good option.) Brick and flagstone will never be as easy to maintain as other countertop options, but they may be the right design choice in rustic settings.

Glazed ceramic tile countertop

Stone slab countertop

Decorative concrete countertop

Flagstone countertop

cooking appliances

The growing popularity of outdoor cooking has inspired a whole new generation of appliances. To check out the latest products, visit an outdoor kitchen store, home improvement center, or patio furniture store that carries a variety of barbecuing products, or look at some of the Web sites listed in the resource guide at the end of this book.

BASIC GRILL

By far the most common cooking appliance is the grill, which has a source of heat below a grate on which you place food to be cooked. With some accessories (see pages 32–33), a grill can serve other functions as well.

BUILT-IN AND STAND-ALONE GRILLS

In most cases, a grill built into a counter is preferable to one that stands on its own, because it is stable and has handy working surfaces on either side. However, if you sometimes like to wow your guests with special grilling done right next to the table, or if you will sometimes transport the grill to a large gathering in a park, you may appreciate the flexibility of a portable stand-alone unit.

It is possible to custom-build a counter around a stand-alone grill, but building the counter may be more complicated and the grill will not have a flange that fits over the counter, making it less stable than a built-in unit.

GAS OR CHARCOAL

Many people prefer to cook with gas (either natural gas or propane) because it is so easy. Just turn on the burner and throw the meat on the grill.

However, a growing number of grillers believe that charcoal produces superior flavor, making a charcoal grill well worth the extra work of starting a fire, waiting for the coals to get hot, and cleaning up afterward. Built-in charcoal units are available, though they are not as common as gas units.

Built-in grill

Stand-alone grill

Some propane grills have an accessory pan that lets you cook with charcoal as well as propane.

GAS GRILLS If you grill only occasionally, or if it is difficult to run a gas line from the house to the grill, you may want to place a liquid propane (LP) tank in the counter below the grill. It is easy to hook up, though you will need to exchange the empty tank for a full one from time to time. With a gas hookup, you will save money in the long run and avoid having to return tanks. Propane and natural gas burn at about the same temperature.

When shopping for a gas grill, look for a sturdy, well-built unit. Pay attention to the warranty, especially in the event of mechanical failures. To ease cleaning,

Infrared grill

look for a removable bottom and a grate that catches and vaporizes drippings.

INFRARED An infrared cooking unit directs intense heat at the food, and so is used with the grill hood open. The high temperature quickly sears food and locks in moisture and flavor.

Manufacturers boast that infrared grills produce twice the flavor in half the time. An infrared burner may be fueled by natural gas, electricity, or propane. You can purchase a stand-alone unit or one that attaches to a standard grill.

CHARCOAL GRILLS A good charcoal grill is typically constructed of powder-coated or porcelain-enameled steel. The grate may be porcelainized or nickel plated, to resist rust and clean up easily, or bare cast iron, which sears meat wonderfully but must be oiled regularly to prevent rusting. In either case, the more closely

Built-in charcoal grill

Drop-in charcoal grill with crank

spaced the bars of the grate, the better. A unit with a crank that lowers and raises the grate will make the heat easier to control.

Check out the grill's ash-removal system to see that it will be easy to get at once the unit is installed. Some grills can close down tightly, which kills the fire and allows you to reuse unburned charcoal. With other units, you have to use all new charcoal each time you cook.

Inexpensive charcoal briquettes are made largely of minerals rather than wood. Many people find that wood charcoal, which is generally irregular in shape and size, imparts a more satisfying flavor. In addition to the charcoal, you can add wood chips of mesquite, hickory, and other species for a distinct flavor.

BURNERS

Gas- or propane-powered burners allow you to fry, boil, and sauté a variety of side dishes, eliminating the need for trips to the indoor kitchen. One common arrangement is to have a large grill plus a small burner unit. You can buy a burner that is specially made for use with a wok.

SMOKERS

Smoked meat has an unmatched flavor. Most smokers are stand-alone units, but built-in smokers are also available.

An egg-shaped kamado cooker can be used as a grill or a smoker. A serious smoker is made of heavy-gauge steel and may be equipped with a motor-driven rotisserie. A smoker on wheels can be carted to picnics when desired.

Side burner

Wok burner

Portable smoker

Grill with side burner

cooking amenities

More and more accessories are available for outdoor kitchens. Here are some of the most common ones.

MAKING IT A REAL KITCHEN

With the addition of a refrigerator and a sink with running water, your outdoor cooking area will be transformed into a fully functioning kitchen.

REFRIGERATOR Many manufacturers make refrigerators for outdoor use. Most units are constructed of stainless steel and have tempered glass shelves. They are front vented, so they can be tucked under a countertop, where they receive some protection from the elements.

SINKS AND FAUCETS A prep sink allows for easy and immediate cleanup. Having running water on site is handy for food preparation as well.

There are no sinks or faucets made specifically for use outdoors, but a variety of products will stand up to the weather. Most outdoor sinks are made of stainless steel, but enameled cast-iron or composite materials will be just as durable. Outdoor sinks tend to be smaller than those indoors. A single-bowl sink, or even a bar sink, is often all you really need.

Any high-quality faucet will work outdoors, though it may need to be repaired or replaced a few years sooner than one on an indoor sink. A "one-touch" faucet, which has a spout that pulls out to become a sprayer, is a popular choice. If you live in an area with freezing winters, be sure to drain the faucet and pipes in late fall.

Large sink with one-touch faucet

Bar sink

Left: Cooking outdoors is more relaxing when all the basics are within easy reach. A handy built-in refrigerator stocked with beverages ensures that guests will touch base with the chef occasionally.

COOKING ACCESSORIES

A wide range of available products can turn a simple grill into a multifunctional cooking center.

ROTISSERIES A motor-operated rotisserie typically fits over a large grill or a fire. See page 17 for a churrasco-style rotisserie. The rotisserie must be plugged into an electrical receptacle, so plan a safe route for the cord. Some rotisseries are designed to be used with certain brands and models of grills.

BEER POULTRY ROASTER Roasting a whole chicken over an open can of beer produces a fine flavor, but the arrangement can be unstable. To use such a roaster,
fill the tray with beer, wine, or fruit juice; insert the infuser into the chicken; and stand the chicken upright in the tray. The bird will cook quickly and will be infused with aromatic juices.

ROAST AND VEGETABLE RACKS These devices keep food away from direct contact with the grill and make it easy to transport. You can find racks for almost anything. For instance, kabob kits include six skewers and a rack that holds them just far enough away from each other. Once the cooking is done, you can carry the whole thing to the table.

SMOKER ATTACHMENT Fill this with the wood chips of your
choice and place it on a gas grill for a charcoallike smoky flavor.

RIB RACK Just the right size for ribs or pieces of chicken, this tool allows you to cook more than would normally fit on the grill.

GRIDDLE Set this stainless-steel tray on a hot grate and you're ready to cook bacon, pancakes, and hash browns like a short-order cook in a restaurant.

GRILL BASKET This is an essential tool if you want to grill fragile food such as fish or sandwiches. It also can be used for vegetables. If you want to close the grill's lid while you cook, choose a basket with a detachable handle.

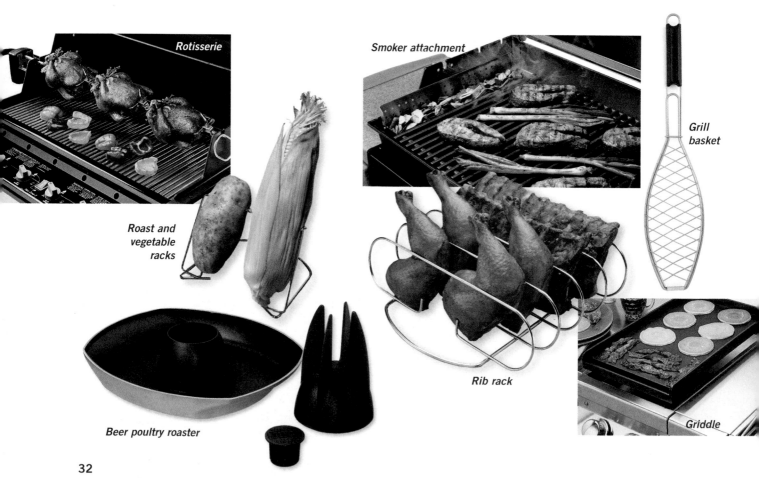

Rotisserie

Smoker attachment

Grill basket

Roast and vegetable racks

Rib rack

Griddle

Beer poultry roaster

UTENSILS AND FINISHING TOUCHES

There are many products on the market that make outdoor cooking more convenient. Also consider accessories that make your kitchen easier to clean and maintain.

THERMOMETER To see that meat is cooked at just the right temperature, poke in a meat thermometer. A remote-control model has a receiving unit that you can carry with you; it will beep when the food is done.

GRILL LIGHT Cooking at night is much more pleasant if you can see what you're doing. You may be able to buy a grill handle with lights or a stand-alone light with a rotating head to shine directly on the grill. Otherwise, buy a light that clamps onto a convenient place. Alternatively, build an overhead with built-in lights that shine on the grill.

GRILL COVERS Protect your appliances with heavy-duty vinyl and cloth covers. They can even prevent water from seeping into cabinets below.

CHIMNEY STARTER Pack the underside with a sheet of newspaper, fill the top with charcoal, and light the newspaper. In 20 minutes or so, the coals will be ready for cooking.

THE RIGHT TOOLS Use long-handled tools—spatula, tongs, or a fork—to pick up and turn meat. (Don't poke the meat with a fork or you'll lose precious juices.) You'll also want a basting brush and a grill-cleaning tool or two.

GRILL HOOD If the grill is near a house, you may need or want to suck cooking smoke up and away. A ventilation hood made for outdoor use will survive damp weather, but you will probably need to keep it protected from direct rainfall.

SLIDE-OUT TANK TRAY This makes changing a propane tank easy and safe.

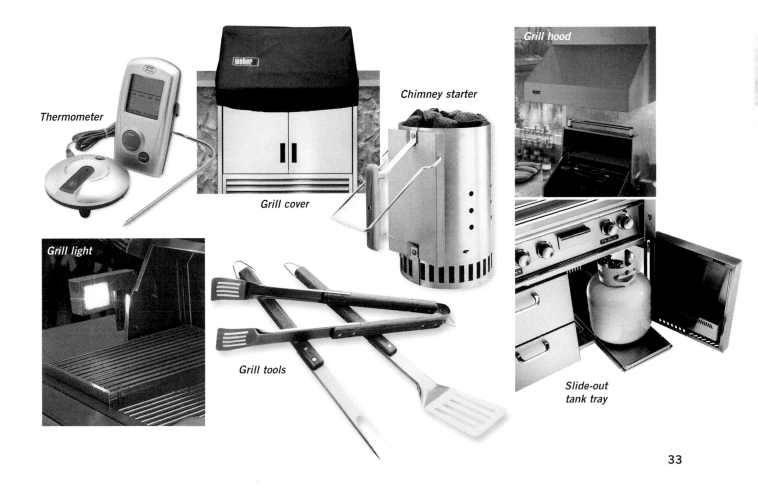

Thermometer

Grill light

Grill cover

Grill tools

Chimney starter

Grill hood

Slide-out tank tray

comfort systems

Left: An energy-efficient overhead heater warms the eating area of this outdoor space. Infrared quartz units like this one add almost instantaneous heat with modest electrical output. Many units plug into a standard 120-volt outlet. *Below:* This popular propane patio heater looks like a floor lamp and generates a warm red glow of infrared heat at the top, fueled by the propane tank at the base. Some models also have wheels.

Outdoor life often means contending with heat, cold, and bugs. While you don't want to make the outdoors feel just like the indoors, there are products available to make you much more comfortable.

HEATERS

You can make a patio a warm retreat on cold evenings. If the patio is fairly small and sheltered from the wind, or if it is tucked up against the house, simply running the grill can do a lot to make things comfortable. A fire pit also offers warmth and creates a cozy illuminated area.

You can also choose from among products designed to make the outdoors warm. All these devices work best when the air is still, as even a small breeze will greatly inhibit their effectiveness. A portable stand-up patio heater typically uses propane. It has a sturdy base with a hatlike reflector on top that disperses the flame's warmth over a surprisingly large area.

An infrared heater installed overhead directs heat toward a fairly limited area. Point one at a seating area. Most use standard 120-volt electrical current. Depending on the size of the unit and your electrical system, you may be able to simply plug it into a receptacle, or you may need to run cable to the service panel and install a new circuit.

For a lower-tech solution, consider an inexpensive outdoor wood-burning fireplace. Old-fashioned-looking models are made of cast iron or clay, while modern-looking versions are generally made of powder-finished steel.

MISTERS

If you live in an area with hot, dry summers, consider a system that sprays a cool and refreshing mist. Type "patio mister" into an Internet search engine to find several companies that make easy-to-install systems.

A kit that includes at least 20 feet of hose and 10 to 15 nozzles can attach to an overhead structure, generating a gentle spray over a large area. Or you can buy a fan that attaches to a garden hose and directs a heavier mist at a more defined area. A misting umbrella provides both shade and humidity for people seated beneath.

*Above left: A charming cast-iron wood-burning unit provides heat and the timeless appeal of an open fire to a patio. **Above:** A misting umbrella hooked up to a garden hose covers the area with a fine spray to bring relief from sweltering heat to both humans and plants.*

DEBUGGING STRATEGIES

There are certain times of the year when bugs might discourage you from using your outdoor kitchen. The Environmental Protection Agency makes the following recommendations for reducing mosquito bites.

- Look out for places where water can collect in your yard: old tires, buckets, plastic covers, toys, etc. Fill temporary pools with dirt, and make sure rain gutters are unclogged.
- Spray your yard with a short-lived insecticide during peak periods of mosquito flight, often around dusk. (Keep in mind that the spray can damage populations of desirable insects and contaminate garden crops.)
- Wear a repellant that contains deet.

drawing up the plan

Once you've decided on the basic contours and appliances for your outdoor kitchen, it's time to draw a precise plan. Consult your local building department, which may have very specific requirements for a written plan. If you need to run plumbing, gas, or electrical lines, or if the structure will be heavy masonry, you almost certainly will need a permit. Check with your building department even if you are installing a modest counter.

ENLISTING HELP

If you feel your drafting skills aren't strong enough, are not sure of the best arrangement, or simply want some new ideas, consider hiring a pro to help with planning and drawing.

If your design is complex or the kitchen will be housed in a separate structure, such as a covered pergola, consider hiring a landscape architect. A licensed architect is technically trained and probably has good working relationships with local contractors, so he or she can supervise every aspect of the job. Hiring a landscape architect may be pricey, but it can be worth the expense if you don't want to oversee the whole project.

If you want to do much of the planning and building yourself, consider hiring a landscape designer, who will be less expensive than a landscape architect. He or she can help with the design, make drawings, help you deal with the permit process, and make plant recommendations.

LAYOUT PRINCIPLES

Indoor kitchen layout follows the "work triangle" principle, which states that the space connecting the stove, sink, and refrigerator should form a triangle, and that each leg of the triangle should be between 4 and 8 feet long. The basic idea is good: The cooking and cleaning appliances should be within easy reach of each other without getting in each other's way. However, outdoor kitchens present more variables, and taking a few more steps is not considered inconvenient, so design is more relaxed. Here are some things to keep in mind.

- Outdoor cooking is often a communal experience, so your plans should include plenty of room for family members and friends to hang out around the cooking fires. An island or peninsula, rather than a counter up against the house, makes face-to-face conversation easier.
- Allow for both small and large dining groups. Perhaps place an eating counter with four stools next to the grill so you can cook and eat together. Plan a separate table for parties.
- Leave enough space for cooking, dining, and traffic. A dining area includes the table plus

36 to 48 inches for chairs on all sides. Leave at least a 6-by-8-foot space around the grill for a cook plus a couple of advisers. In addition, make sure there are 3-foot-wide pathways from one area to the next and from the outdoor kitchen to the house.

- Make sure all the drawers and doors will open without bumping into each other or creating a traffic jam.
- Start to plan for the overhead (see pages 150–153).
- If you have space, consider having more than one outdoor "room." For instance, locating a fire pit or a lounging area even 20 feet from the main dining area can create a place that feels separate.
- Plan how you will keep the area clean. If you are putting in a new patio, pitch it toward a drain so you can spray it clean. Place a sink where people are most likely to use it.

SOME TYPICAL LAYOUTS

Here are three of the most common types of layout.

BASIC COUNTER With a minimum of 7 linear feet (8 will be a bit more comfortable), you can install a counter with a grill and perhaps a bar sink, leaving you with a modest but usable amount of countertop area. You'll have room below for a refrigerator and one or two small doors or drawer units. The counter should be at least 30 inches deep. A counter

that runs along the house wall will be the easiest to build. For more usable space, place the counter so it is an island or a peninsula perpendicular to the house, and widen the countertop to 48 inches.

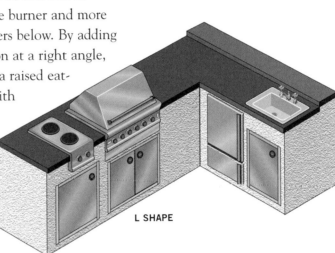

BASIC COUNTER

L SHAPE This is often an ideal choice when you must build against the house. Lengthening the counter to 10 feet leaves room for a side burner and more doors or drawers below. By adding another section at a right angle, you can have a raised eating counter with stools on the other side. The sink is positioned within easy reach of diners.

L SHAPE

U SHAPE This design gives you three distinct areas for food preparation, grilling, and eating. Either the sink side or the grill side may be attached to the house. Though it takes up only about 100 square feet

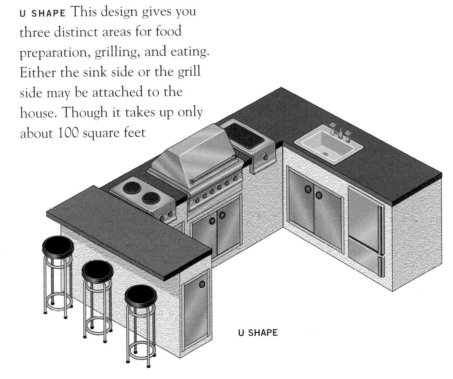

U SHAPE

(leaving room for the stools), you'll have space for a full sink, three cooking appliances, a refrigerator, and plenty of storage below. The area within the U is just large enough for two or three people to cook without bumping into each other.

LAYOUTS FOR LARGE KITCHENS
Most elaborate outdoor kitchens have surprisingly simple designs. The counters and ovens are often arranged in a straight line or in an L shape, as shown at right. Sometimes a fireplace or oven with a counter is built separately, perhaps 20 feet away and facing the main counter.

DRAWING A PLAN

Time spent making and revising drawn plans will almost certainly pay for itself in work saved later. A set of detailed and accurate plans will help you execute your design with fewer mistakes. The process of drawing plans will help you spot and solve problems ahead of time. It may also help you think of ways to save in materials and labor.

You need only a few simple drafting tools. With a transparent drafting ruler, you can quickly measure and draw parallel lines. Use a compass to draw curves and figure a radius. You'll probably need a calculator for figuring materials. Or use your computer. Some word processing programs have simple design applications.

BASE PLAN Start with a drawing of the yard that covers an area somewhat larger than the kitchen. If you have a survey drawing for your lot, you can enlarge a portion of it. If you have no survey, measure the area and make an accurate drawing, including any permanent plantings. Graph paper often helps keep things to scale. Make five or six photocopies of this base plan so that you can experiment with different designs and throw out rejected plans.

PLAN VIEW AND ELEVATION On a photocopied base plan, draw a plan view, also called an overhead view. Be precise in all your measurements and double-check everything.

An elevation is a side-view drawing. You will likely need to make several to show all sides of the project. Draw it at the same scale as the plan view. Use literature from appliance manufacturers to sketch what the grills and other appliances will look like.

An elevation drawing will likely show the below-ground substructure. If your project is being inspected by your local building department, inspectors will be very interested in this aspect of the drawings. Be sure to find out what their requirements are for supporting counters and ovens, and show the inspector that you will comply.

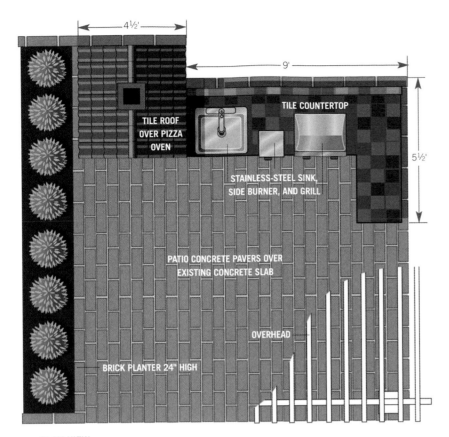

4½'

9'

TILE COUNTERTOP

TILE ROOF
OVER PIZZA
OVEN

5½'

STAINLESS-STEEL SINK,
SIDE BURNER, AND GRILL

PATIO CONCRETE PAVERS OVER
EXISTING CONCRETE SLAB

OVERHEAD

BRICK PLANTER 24" HIGH

PLAN VIEW

OVERHEAD If you will build an overhead, the inspector may or may not want to see detailed plans. Because the overhead covers at least part of the kitchen, just generally indicate its location on the plan and elevation drawings and make a separate detailed drawing for the overhead.

MATERIALS LIST As you draw, list all the materials you will need. The inspector will want to know specific information about structural elements like concrete reinforcement. The list will aid you greatly during construction.

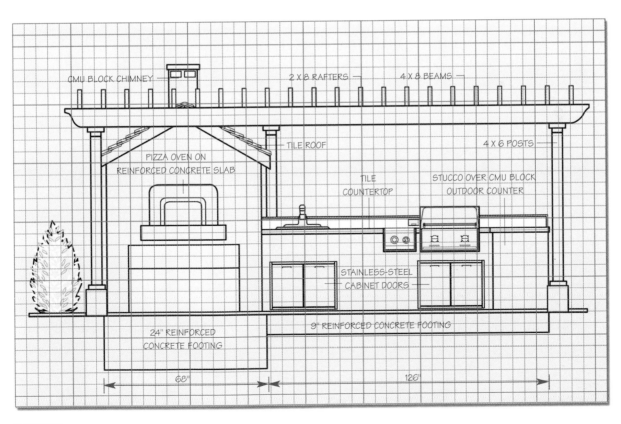

CMU BLOCK CHIMNEY

2 X 8 RAFTERS

4 X 8 BEAMS

PIZZA OVEN ON
REINFORCED CONCRETE SLAB

TILE ROOF

4 X 6 POSTS

TILE
COUNTERTOP

STUCCO OVER CMU BLOCK
OUTDOOR COUNTER

STAINLESS-STEEL
CABINET DOORS

24" REINFORCED
CONCRETE FOOTING

9" REINFORCED CONCRETE FOOTING

68"

126"

ELEVATION

barbecue projects

IN THIS CHAPTER YOU WILL FIND 16 PLANS for building all types of barbecues and outdoor kitchens, as well as some overhead structures to provide shade. Each project includes a photograph of the finished kitchen, illustrations that show how it was put together, and basic step-by-step building instructions. A materials list for each project specifies the primary materials you will need. You will most likely need to adapt the plans to suit your particular yard, budget, needs, and tastes, so quantities and sizes of materials are not specified in most instances. Study the plans carefully to decide whether you want to tackle all or part of the project yourself, or hire a pro. The instructions will direct you at various points to pages in Chapter 3, where you will find more detailed guidance on specific building techniques. As you firm up your plans, be aware that local building codes may apply.

cobblestone counter with granite

This outdoor kitchen is straightforward yet eye-catching. The counter is subtly curved and appears to be covered with open-jointed stone, which makes it resemble a rustic stone wall. The stones, which are actually faux, or cultured, pick up many of the colors in the patio's flagstones below. The granite countertop gives the impression of a 4-inch-thick slab. Though expensive, granite is a great choice for an outdoor countertop because it is extremely durable and easy to keep clean.

Positioned along the yard's perimeter, this design adds a gentle curve to a basic rectangular counter. DESIGN: KAREN AITKEN & ASSOCIATES

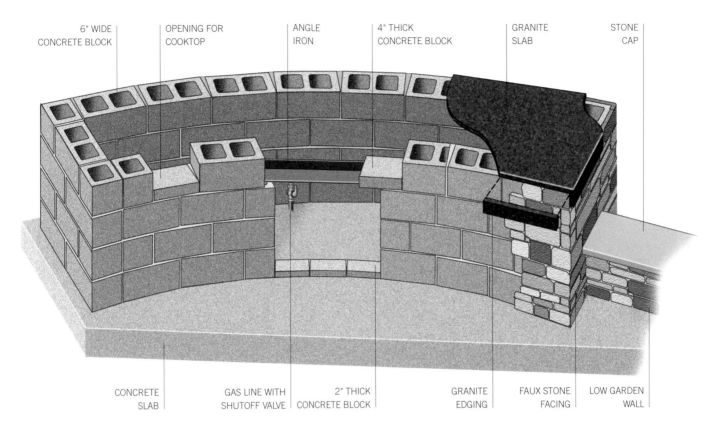

6" WIDE
CONCRETE BLOCK

OPENING FOR
COOKTOP

ANGLE
IRON

4" THICK
CONCRETE BLOCK

GRANITE
SLAB

STONE
CAP

CONCRETE
SLAB

GAS LINE WITH
SHUTOFF VALVE

2" THICK
CONCRETE BLOCK

GRANITE
EDGING

FAUX STONE
FACING

LOW GARDEN
WALL

TO SUPPORT THE GRILL, SEE PAGES 106–107

THE DESIGN

The counter is curved very gently —only 4 inches over a span of 11 feet—but this slight deviation has a surprisingly large visual impact. A rectangular counter would have a very different feel.

While the counter is curved, the countertop is rectangular, meaning that the top overhangs the counter more in some places than in others. The grill is located front and center—one of the places where the overhang is most pronounced—thereby de-emphasizing the difference in shape between the counter and the countertop.

The homeowners were aiming for a pristine, uncluttered effect, so there is only one door, directly below the large grill. This limits usable storage space, but many people find the area below an outdoor counter to be an awkward place to reach. If you want to add storage while limiting the amount of visible stainless steel, consider installing doors on the rear of the unit.

The only utility line is gas pipe for the grill and the side burner. If you choose propane-fired appliances, you would not have to run any utility lines. If you want to hook up a rotisserie or plug in small electrical appliances, run electrical conduit and install GFCI receptacles (see pages 108–109, 142–143).

A reinforced concrete slab supports the structure and forms the floor inside the unit. The walls are built of 6-inch concrete. A structure like this could also be

43

built with wood framing and concrete backerboard (see pages 124–125). The top and bottom pieces would need to be bent into curves, which is not difficult to do with wood. It would not be practical to build a curved counter using steel studs. The blocks are faced with faux stone, which comes in a wide variety of colors and shapes and is fairly easy to install. You could also cover the counter with tile or stucco (see pages 130–131 and 126–127).

The granite slab counter in this project is actually $1\frac{1}{2}$ inches thick. A $2\frac{1}{2}$-inch-wide strip of granite under the edges makes the slab appear to be 4 inches thick. The grill and the side burner are both high-end stainless-steel models that will provide years of reliable service and will allow for easy cleanup.

On the right, the counter is attached to a low garden wall. The wall is constructed of concrete block covered with faux stone and is capped with 1-inch-thick stone.

GETTING READY

Read through the building instructions and relevant sections of Chapter 3 to determine whether you will handle the installation yourself. Pouring the footing, building the block walls, and covering them with stone are all within the capabilities of a handy and strong homeowner. Installing the granite top, however, is best left to specialists.

Before you begin work, buy the cooking units and the door. Find the sizes for all the rough openings and draw your plans carefully to be sure everything will fit. Don't forget to take into account the thickness of the countertop. Have the units on site when you build so you can periodically check that they will fit.

Plan the placement of all the blocks. Unless you have a prescribed space in which the unit must fit, you should be able to plan the installation to minimize the cutting of blocks. Consult the granite company when you plan the building of the walls to make sure that the cooking units will fit after the granite is installed.

MATERIALS LIST

- Grill
- Two-burner cooktop
- Outdoor cabinet doors
- Gas pipe, shutoff valve, and connections
- Concrete for the footing
- Concrete block
- Steel reinforcing bar
- Mortar mix
- 3" × 5" angle iron
- Faux stone for facing
- Granite slab for the countertop
- Silicone caulk

1 Excavate, Run the Gas Line, and Pour Concrete

The perimeter of the footing is 8 inches wide and 12 inches thick (see bottom illustration, opposite page), but check with your local building department to make sure you comply with its codes, which may call for a much thicker footing. Excavate and build forms (see pages 108–111). Run the gas line into the area and install a T fitting and stubouts so you can provide gas for both cooking units. Install horizontal reinforcing bar as required by code. If you will fill the block cells with concrete, also run vertical rebar, carefully placed so it will run up through every other cell. Pour and finish the footing.

2 Build the Block Walls

To plan for a gently curved wall, you could make a compass using a long string attached to a stake somewhere in the yard. For a simpler solution, chalk a straight line on the footing, then arrange the first row of blocks in a dry run. Place the center block or blocks 4 inches from the mark and position the other blocks progressively closer to the line (see top illustration, opposite page). Stand back and eyeball the arrangement and make adjustments as needed. Then use a pencil to mark the positions of the blocks.

After allowing the slab to cure for several days, build the block walls (see pages 114–117). At the door opening, install an angle iron and place 4-inch block. See pages 106–107 for planning this opening, which needs to be carefully sized. If the grill requires them, build a solid support and an enclosure.

CREATING THE CURVE

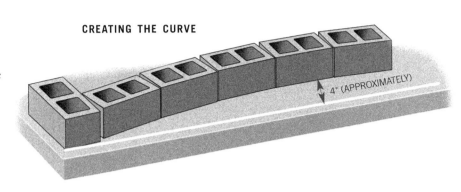

4" (APPROXIMATELY)

3 Face with Faux Stone

Faux stones are easy to cut and install, and the corner pieces make it simple to produce a clean look. See pages 128–129 for installation instructions. Apply mortar to the block wall using a notched trowel and set the stones in the mortar. You may need to use temporary spacers to keep the stones from sliding down while the mortar is wet. In this installation, the joints are not mortared.

4 Have the Granite Slab Installed

Once the counter is built, have the granite company come out and measure for the countertop. You may have to wait several weeks for installation. Discuss how you want the edges to be finished. In this case, an edging piece was installed just below the slab and the edge was ground and polished to look like a monolithic piece of granite. Granite is impervious to most stains, but you may still want to apply a sealer for extra protection.

SIDE VIEW

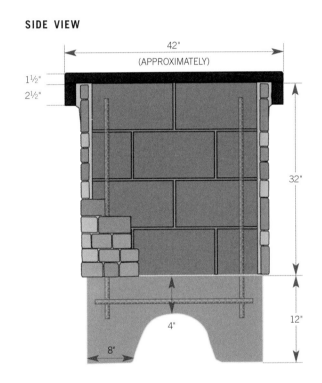

42" (APPROXIMATELY)
1½"
2½"
32"
12"
4"
8"

5 Install the Appliances and the Door

Hook up the burner and the grill to the gas line. Apply silicone caulk to seal the appliances and then install them in the openings (see pages 148–149). Apply caulk to and install the door.

barbecue bar

The basic idea here is obvious at a glance: Guests sit at stools on one side of the counter while the cook acts as master of ceremonies on the other, barbecuing and serving up the food much like a chef at a Japanese grill restaurant. The handsomely massive granite countertop brings everyone together in a friendly dining atmosphere. The winged shape and the ample width of the counter are carefully chosen to create intimacy without a feeling of claustrophobia. The counter has plenty of space for setting out buffet items as well as tableware. The counter was designed to blend in with its surroundings.

The same stones are used on the nearby wall, the granite countertop is an attractive neutral shade, and the grill is only partly visible from most vantage points.

THE DESIGN

The countertop is symmetrical, with two wings each at an angle to the central section. On the cooking side, each section is 6 feet long. The countertop overhangs the counter by 3 inches on the ends and on the cooking side, and it cantilevers out 12 inches on the dining side for comfortable seating. The grill is placed in the center of the cooking side.

The granite slab counter is $1\frac{1}{2}$ inches thick. At the edges, a strip

Reminiscent of a bar at a vacation spot, this barbecue also offers enough grill and countertop space to produce a full scale meal. DESIGN: KAREN AITKEN & ASSOCIATES

of granite is installed underneath to give the appearance of being 4 inches thick. You could choose instead to install a countertop made of tile, decorative concrete, or slab stone (see pages 132–139).

There is only one appliance, a high-quality grill large enough to handle several cooking tasks at once. The grill is fueled by propane, so there is no need to run a gas line. (If you prefer natural gas, see pages 108–109 and 140–141.) Two electrical receptacles, located on the cooking side of the counter, supply power for small appliances or a rotisserie.

A reinforced concrete slab supports the structure and forms the floor inside the unit. The walls are built of 6-inch concrete block. A structure like this could also be built with wood or steel framing and concrete backerboard (see pages 122–125). The blocks are faced with faux stone, which comes in a wide variety of colors and shapes and is fairly easy to install. The joints between the stones are filled with mortar.

GETTING READY

Pouring the footing, building the block walls, and covering

them with faux stone are all within the capabilities of a handy and strong homeowner. Applying the faux stones is not difficult, but it will take some practice to learn how to fill and tool the

joints. Installing the granite top is definitely best left to granite specialists.

Before you begin work, buy the grill and the doors and make sure everything will fit. When figuring the openings for the cooking units, don't forget to take into account the thickness of the countertop. Have the units on site when you build so you can periodically check their fit.

Plan the placement of all the blocks. Unless you have a prescribed space into which the unit must fit, you should be able to plan the installation to minimize the cutting of blocks. Consult the granite company when you plan the building of the walls to make sure that the cooking units will fit after the granite is installed.

THE SUBSTRUCTURE

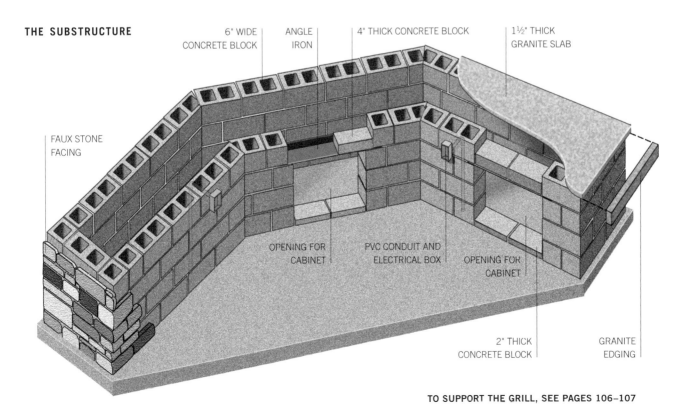

6" WIDE CONCRETE BLOCK

ANGLE IRON

4" THICK CONCRETE BLOCK

1½" THICK GRANITE SLAB

FAUX STONE FACING

OPENING FOR CABINET

PVC CONDUIT AND ELECTRICAL BOX

OPENING FOR CABINET

2" THICK CONCRETE BLOCK

GRANITE EDGING

TO SUPPORT THE GRILL, SEE PAGES 106–107

1 Excavate, Run the Electrical Lines, and Pour Concrete

The footing for this project is 8 inches wide and 24 inches thick, but check with your local building department to make sure you comply with its codes. Excavate and build forms (see pages 108–111). Run electrical conduit for the receptacles. Install horizontal reinforcing bar as required by code. If you will fill the block cells with concrete, also run vertical rebar, carefully placed so it will run up through every other cell. Pour and finish the footing.

2 Build the Block Walls

After allowing the slab to cure for several days, build the block walls (see pages 114–117). At the door opening, install angle irons and then 2-inch block on top. See pages 106–107 for planning this opening, which needs to be carefully sized. If the grill requires them, build a solid support and an enclosure.

3 Face with Faux Stone

See pages 128–129 for instructions on installing stones. Apply mortar to the block wall using a notched trowel, then set the stones in the mortar. You may need to use temporary spacers to keep the stones from sliding down while the mortar is wet. Fill the joints with mortar and tool them.

4 Have the Granite Slab Installed

Once the counter is built, have the granite company come out and measure for the countertop. The edges should be smoothed and polished so they shine like the rest of the countertop. Granite is impervious to most stains, but you may want to apply a sealer anyway for extra protection.

5 Install the Appliances and Door

Hook up the grill to the gas line. Apply silicone caulk to seal the flange, then install the grill in the opening (see pages 140–141 and 148–149). Install the doors and apply caulk to seal out rain.

DIMENSIONS

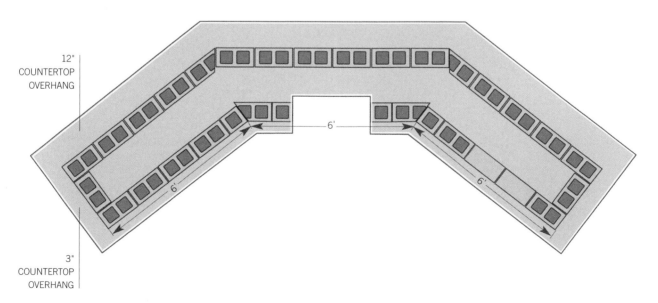

12"
COUNTERTOP
OVERHANG

6'

6'

6'

3"
COUNTERTOP
OVERHANG

brick and tile counter

This classic counter has a large grill plus a two-burner cooktop so the chef can heat a couple of side dishes while barbecuing. The counter is faced with common brick that is manufactured to look used. The countertop is covered with light-colored ceramic tile.

THE DESIGN

This is a straightforward masonry counter with two openings for appliances on top and two doors below. A reinforced concrete slab supports the structure and forms the floor inside the unit. The walls are made of 6-inch concrete block that is faced with brick. This counter has only about 4 feet of usable counter space. If your yard has more room, you may choose to lengthen the counter you build.

The tiled countertop has a distinctly massive appearance due to the wide edging pieces in front and the 4-inch backsplash. The substructure for this 3-inch-thick countertop is made of ½-inch concrete backerboard topped with a 2-inch layer of reinforced concrete. If you do not want wide edging pieces, install metal-stud braces every 16 inches or so and use layers of backerboard to build the substructure (see page 132). The backsplash is made with 4-inch-thick block, which makes it deep enough to serve as a shelf for potted plants.

This simple, straightforward counter unit houses a grill, a side burner, and two storage areas, making it ready to handle both the main course and side dishes.
DESIGN: RANSOHOFF, BLANCHFIELD, JONES, INC. LANDSCAPE ARCHITECTS

GETTING READY

Building a finished-looking brick wall calls for good masonry skills. If you do not have experience, you may choose to hire a pro for this aspect of the job.

Buy the grill, cooktop, and doors and have them on hand as you build so that you can be sure everything will fit. Buy an ensemble of countertop tiles, including bullnose pieces for the front edge and the top of the backsplash, and perhaps special corner pieces.

1 Excavate, Run the Gas Line, and Pour Concrete

Excavate and build forms for a footing and slab that will support a heavy masonry structure and meet local building codes (see pages 108–111). The perimeter footing of the unit shown is 8 inches wide and 2 feet deep. Run the gas line into this area. If you want electrical receptacles, run an electrical line as well. Pour and finish the footing.

2 Build the Block Walls

After allowing the slab to cure for several days, build the block walls (see pages 114–117). You do not need to install angle irons and blocks over the door openings; you'll do that when you build the brick wall. Check that the cooking units and doors will fit before moving on.

MATERIALS LIST

- Grill
- Two-burner cooktop
- Outdoor cabinet doors
- Gas pipe, shutoff valve, and connections
- Concrete block
- Steel reinforcing bar
- Mortar mix
- Common brick
- 3" angle irons
- ½" concrete backerboard
- Sand-mix concrete for the countertop substrate
- 2 × 4s for concrete forms
- Countertop tile
- Thinset mortar
- Grout
- Silicone caulk for sealing doors and appliances

3 Face with Brick

Lay a brick wall up against the block wall (see pages 118–121). Use the same techniques as for a block wall, but take special care to maintain straight lines. Apply mortar not only to the bricks but to the block wall as well, and adhere the bricks to the blocks. Over the door openings, install angle irons and lay bricks on top of them. Strike and clean the joints as you go.

4 Build the Countertop Substrate

Cut pieces of ½-inch concrete backerboard for the countertop base so that their edges extend to the outside of the brick walls. Check to be sure the cooking units will fit, trowel a layer of mortar onto the top of the blocks and bricks, and lay the backerboard on top. Check for level in both directions. Inside the counter, temporarily support the backerboard by propping 2 by 4s every 16 inches or so. Build 2-by-4 forms around the perimeter of the backerboard (see pages 136–139). Make a stiff batch of sand-mix concrete and cast a 2-inch-thick slab. Trowel the surface smooth.

5 Set the Tiles

When the concrete has cured, remove the forms. Set the tiles, following instructions on pages 132–135. Lay the tiles in a dry run, make the cuts, and set the tiles in reinforced thinset mortar. Use bullnose tiles on the front and side edges and on top of the backsplash. Wait a day for the mortar to harden, then apply grout and wipe clean.

6 Install the Cooking Units and Doors

Hook up the gas valve and run lines for the grill and the cooktop (see pages 140–141). Set the grill and the cooktop and make the connections below. Install the doors (see page 149).

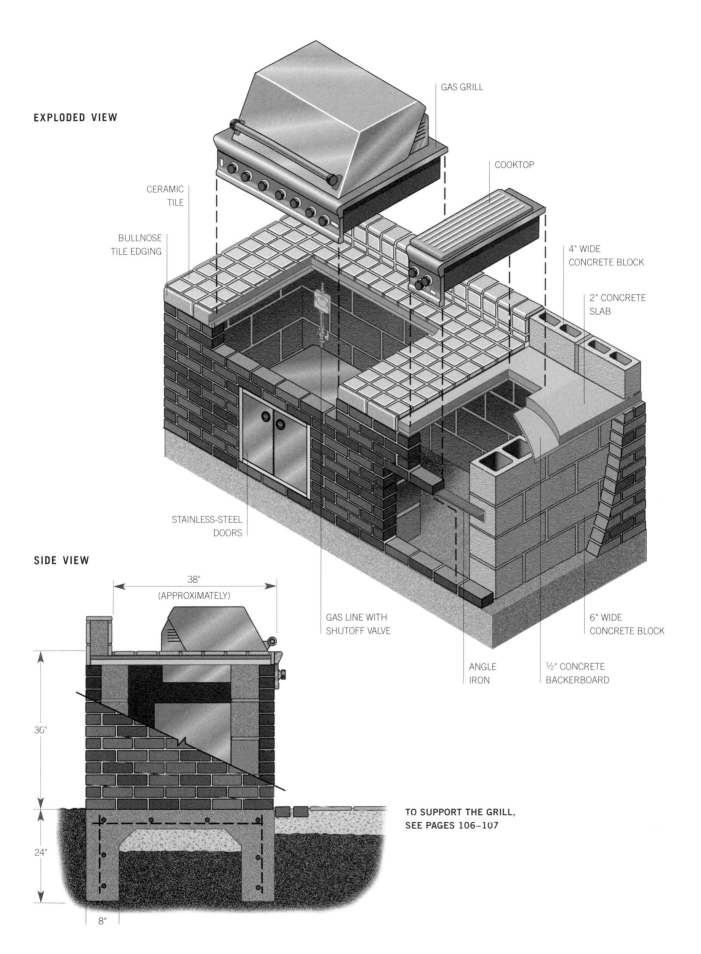

EXPLODED VIEW

GAS GRILL

COOKTOP

CERAMIC
TILE

BULLNOSE
TILE EDGING

4" WIDE
CONCRETE BLOCK

2" CONCRETE
SLAB

STAINLESS-STEEL
DOORS

SIDE VIEW

38"
(APPROXIMATELY)

GAS LINE WITH
SHUTOFF VALVE

6" WIDE
CONCRETE BLOCK

36"

ANGLE
IRON

½" CONCRETE
BACKERBOARD

**TO SUPPORT THE GRILL,
SEE PAGES 106–107**

24"

8"

tile and stone beauty

With its salmon-toned countertop tiles and boulderlike natural stones covering the counter, this kitchen has an earthy feel. Yet it doesn't scrimp on modern amenities, which include a large grill with electric rotisserie, a gas side burner, overhead lighting, and a refrigerator. An overhead structure adds a moderate amount of shade and gives the outdoor kitchen a finished look.

THE DESIGN

The stones used here are 6 to 7 inches thick and are only partially squared off. Stones like these, which are commonly used to build walls or pillars, may be found at a stone yard under the name "semidressed stone," "coursed rubble," or "quarried wall stone." The same stones are used for the pillars in the yard, and the patio flagstones are similarly colored. Many of the stones are gray, as is the mortar. This causes the stainless-steel appliances and doors to blend visually.

The counter is made of two portions that are at a slight angle to each other. This helps make the counter feel more free-form than geometric.

Because it was built in California's earthquake-conscious Bay Area, the counter's 6-inch

A wide V-angle lends a casual, open feel to this generous counter unit, which houses a grill, side burner, and refrigerator.
DESIGN: RANSOHOFF, BLANCHFIELD, JONES, INC.

THE SUBSTRUCTURE

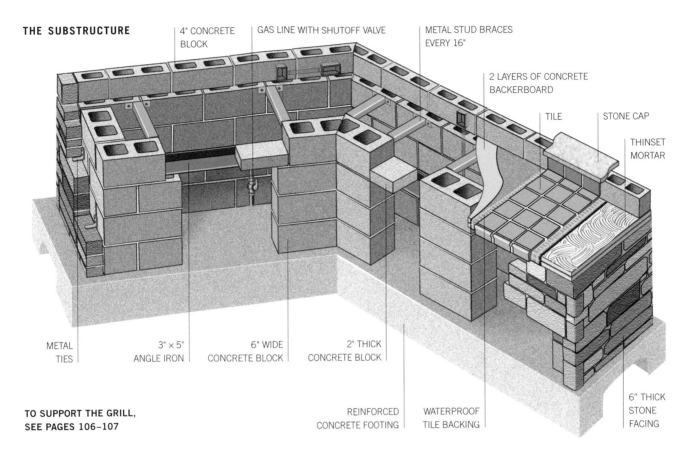

4" CONCRETE BLOCK

GAS LINE WITH SHUTOFF VALVE

METAL STUD BRACES EVERY 16"

2 LAYERS OF CONCRETE BACKERBOARD

TILE

STONE CAP

THINSET MORTAR

METAL TIES

3" × 5" ANGLE IRON

6" WIDE CONCRETE BLOCK

2" THICK CONCRETE BLOCK

REINFORCED CONCRETE FOOTING

WATERPROOF TILE BACKING

6" THICK STONE FACING

TO SUPPORT THE GRILL, SEE PAGES 106–107

concrete blocks are reinforced with vertical rebar and their cells are filled with concrete (see pages 99–100). Add large stones to the facing and you can be sure this structure will be intact for decades. A structure this heavy calls for a massive concrete slab (see pages 110–111).

Stones this thick are not simply adhered to the block wall, as the thinner facing stones are. They must be stacked and mortared together like a stone wall. Corrugated metal ties help anchor the stones to the block wall. The back side of the counter (not visible in photo) is covered with stucco rather than stone.

Because a large tree supplies shade during the afternoon, only

a modest overhead structure was needed. This design supplies a bit of noontime shade and adds a handsome decorative touch.

The overhead is built of redwood, stained to harmonize with the yard's fence.

MATERIALS LIST

FOR THE COUNTER:
- Grill
- Two-burner cooktop
- Outdoor cabinet doors
- Gas pipe, shutoff valve, and connections
- Concrete for the footing
- Concrete block
- Steel reinforcing bar
- Mortar mix
- 3" × 5" angle iron
- Stone for facing
- Corrugated metal wall ties
- Stucco mix
- ½" concrete backerboard

- Waterproof tile backing
- Countertop tile
- Cut stone for the backsplash ledge
- Thinset mortar
- Fortified grout
- Grout sealer
- Silicone caulk

FOR THE OVERHEAD:
- 6 × 6s for posts
- Concrete for the postholes
- 2 × 10s for the beams
- 4 × 4s for the rafters
- 2 × 2s for the top pieces
- 9" bolts with nuts and washers
- 3" deck screws

GETTING READY

Building a stone wall like this calls for good stonemasonry skills. If you are inexperienced, you may choose to cover the block with facing stones (see pages 128–129) or stucco (see pages 126–127).

The overhead could be built after the counter is finished, but it will save work to at least dig the postholes and install the posts at the same time as you excavate for the footing.

Buy the grill, side burner, and doors and have them on hand as you work so that you can be sure everything will fit. Buy an ensemble of tiles, including V-cap or bullnose pieces for the front edge, and perhaps corner pieces.

THE COUNTER

1 Excavate, Run the Lines, and Pour the Concrete

Excavate and build forms for a footing and slab that will support a heavy masonry structure and meet local building codes (see pages 108–111). The perimeter footing should support both the blocks and the stones. This footing is 12 inches wide and 16 inches deep. Run the gas line so it will emerge inside the counter. Then lay the electrical conduit into the area. (You will need a receptacle inside the counter for the refrigerator, as well as receptacles on the counter's backsplash.) Install steel reinforcement for the footing and, if you will fill the cells with concrete, vertical rebar that will run up through the cells of the blocks.

2 Build the Block Walls

After allowing the slab to cure for several days, build the block walls (see pages 114–117). Use 6-inch block for most of the walls and 4-by-4-inch block for the backsplash. Over the doorways, install angle irons and mortar 2-inch solid blocks on top. Run the electrical conduit up through the blocks and install electrical boxes on the backsplash. For added strength, fill the cells of the blocks with concrete.

3 Build the Abutting Stone Walls

On the two sides and the front, choose and/or cut stones to fit in the space and to stack neatly on top of each other. Aim for mortar joints that are fairly consistent in width. This is a slow process involving a great deal of trial and error. Once you have four or five stones prepared, mix a stiff batch of mortar. Apply mortar to the concrete footing and the block wall and then set the bottom stones. Nail corrugated metal wall ties to the block and bend them so they rest on the tops of the stones. Apply more mortar and continue stacking stones. When the mortar is hard enough to retain a thumbprint, tool the joints. Check that the doors and cooking units will fit. Apply stucco to the rear side of the counter (see pages 126–127).

4 Apply the Backerboard

Cut pieces of metal framing (see pages 122–123) to span across the block wall and support the tile backerboard. Cut so that there are 2-inch-long tabs, and anchor the tabs to the backerboard by drilling holes and driving masonry screws. Cut backerboard pieces so they will overhang the stones by about an inch. Check that the cooking units will fit, then cut pieces for a second layer of backerboard and set it in a bed of thinset mortar.

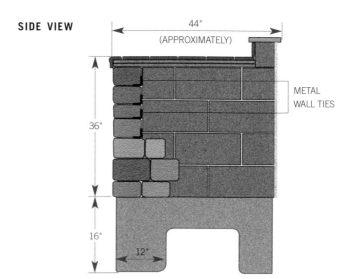

SIDE VIEW

44"
(APPROXIMATELY)

36"

16"

12"

METAL
WALL TIES

5 Set the Tiles and the Ledge

Lay the countertop tiles following the methods shown on pages 132–135. Starting with the V-cap at the edges, set all the tiles in a dry run and make any needed cuts. Also cut tiles for the backsplash. Then lay one section at a time in thinset mortar. Set the cut stone in mortar on top of the backsplash ledge. Wait for the mortar to harden, then grout.

6 Install the Appliances

Run electrical lines and hook up the receptacles as shown on pages 142–143. Install a gas shutoff valve and flexible lines. Then set and install the grill and the side burner (see pages 140–141 and 148–149). Attach the doors and plug in the refrigerator. After a week or so, apply a coat of sealer to the grout and perhaps to the stones and mortar as well.

THE OVERHEAD

1 Set the Three Posts

See pages 150–153 for general instructions on building an overhead. The drawing above (top) shows the orientation of the 6-by-6 posts. The two outside posts are oriented so that one side is parallel to the counter, and the center post is oriented so that one side faces the corner. Set the posts in postholes and temporarily brace them, but do not pour concrete until the overhead is completed. This will allow you to adjust the posts as you work.

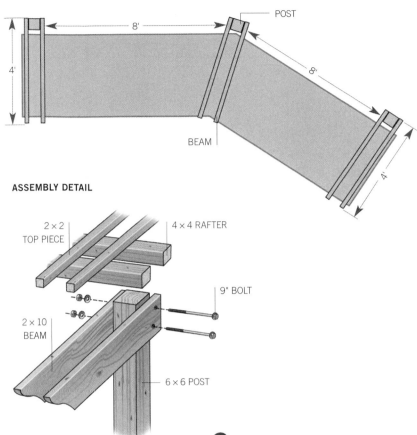

ORIENTATION OF POSTS AND BEAMS

POST

8'

4'

BEAM

8'

4'

ASSEMBLY DETAIL

2 × 2 TOP PIECE

4 × 4 RAFTER

9" BOLT

2 × 10 BEAM

6 × 6 POST

2 Add the Beams

For the side posts, cut four 2-by-10 beams to the same length—about 4 feet. The beams for the center post will need to be slightly longer. Cut them about a foot too long at this point. Using a template, make decorative cuts on the beams' front ends. Mark the posts for the same height—about 8 feet. Attach the beams to the side posts by drilling holes and installing a pair of bolts with washers and nuts. Use screws to temporarily attach the beams to the center post.

3 Add the Rafters and Top Pieces

Cut the 4-by-4 rafters at 15 degrees on one end so that the counter will make a 30-degree turn. Do not cut the pieces to length, as each one will be different. Set the rafters on top of the beams and adjust them so that they are evenly spaced. This will show you how long the middle beams need to be. Take all the pieces down, cut the middle beams to length, and attach the middle beams with bolts. Attach the rafters by drilling angled pilot holes and driving screws into the beams. Cut the 2-by-2 top pieces, space them evenly, and attach them by drilling pilot holes and driving screws into the rafters.

family grilling counter

Above: *When the indoor kitchen is just a window away, two cooks can work together by passing ingredients back and forth.* **Facing page, top:** *The end result: enjoying cooking outdoors with your family.* DESIGNED AND BUILT BY CARL STEFFENS AND FAMILY

Building an outdoor counter may be time-consuming, but if you enjoy building projects and take it slowly it can also be fun. This backyard barbecue was built by a homeowner, with assistance from his two young daughters, over six or seven weekends. The family now has not only an outdoor kitchen that they love to use but also fond memories of its construction.

THE DESIGN

The location of the counter is ideal, both for convenience and for ease of installation. It is placed against the house, just opposite the kitchen sink. This made running the plumbing lines relatively easy, since runs were short and it was possible to tie the drain directly into the kitchen drain (see page 109 for drain options). And because the kitchen window is directly over the counter, it is easy to pass food and dishes in and out. Because the substructure is fairly light, the existing patio was strong enough to support the unit, so the owners did not have to dig and pour a concrete footing. (If you need to pour a footing, see pages 108–111 for instructions.)

The counter has an L shape, with a 7-foot-long working counter attached to the house and a 5½-foot-long eating counter running perpendicular to the house. The eating counter is 42 inches high, while the working counter is a standard 36 inches high. The central working area, which supports the grill, is made of fire-safe concrete block, and the other areas are framed with wood. Backerboard covers the block and wood. The counter's backerboard is covered with stucco, and the countertop is covered with ceramic tile.

THE SUBSTRUCTURE

TO SUPPORT THE GRILL, SEE PAGES 106–107

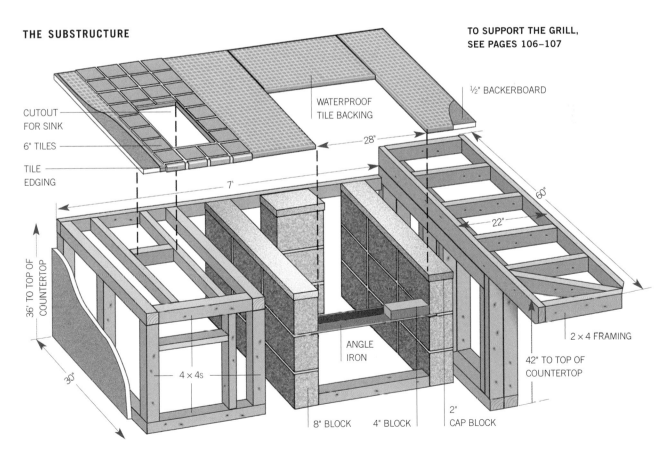

CUTOUT FOR SINK

6" TILES

TILE EDGING

WATERPROOF TILE BACKING

28"

½" BACKERBOARD

7'

60"

22"

36' TO TOP OF COUNTERTOP

30"

4 × 4s

ANGLE IRON

8" BLOCK   4" BLOCK

2" CAP BLOCK

2 × 4 FRAMING

42" TO TOP OF COUNTERTOP

GETTING READY

Both the wood framing and the concrete block installations are straightforward, but you may prefer to build entirely with block, or with wood or steel studs (see pages 114–117, 122–125).

Purchase the grill, sink, and doors before you begin building, and plan to construct the counter walls to fit.

MATERIALS LIST

- Sink with faucet and trap
- Outdoor cabinet doors
- Gas pipe, shutoff valve, and connections
- Plumbing supplies: drain lines, supply lines, stop valves
- Electrical supplies: cable or conduit with wire, boxes, GFCI receptacles
- Concrete block
- Mortar mix
- Pressure-treated 2 × 4s and 4 × 4s
- Nails and screws for building framing and attaching boards to the house
- ½" concrete backerboard
- Stucco mix
- Waterproof tile backing
- Fortified thinset mortar
- Tiles
- Fortified grout
- Grout sealer
- Paint

1 Run the Lines

Draw the outline of the unit on the outside kitchen wall and install a 2-by-4 ledger board and two vertical nailers. Open the wall to gain access to the sink plumbing and work with a plumber to run a code-approved drain line. Either run both cold- and hot-water lines from the inside or run a cold-water line only and install an on-demand water heater in the cabinet. Install one GFCI receptacle for the refrigerator and at least one other about 8 inches above the top of the finished counter. Make sure it will be above the counter's backsplash, and put it in a convenient location for running a blender or other appliance. See pages 142–147 for instructions on electrical and plumbing hookups.

2 Substructure for the Grill

Lay concrete blocks to support the grill (see pages 114–117).

The middle block wall does not need to meet the other two. To get the size right, follow the grill manufacturer's instructions. Also set the grill in place to make sure it will fit. To create a doorway strong enough to support the grill, install an angle iron and lay 2-inch block on top.

3 Frame the Sink Side

Working off of the 2 by 4s that are attached to the wall, frame with pressure-treated 2 by 4s and/or 4 by 4s. Attach the bottom framing pieces to the patio by drilling holes and driving masonry screws. Frame the opening for the door and then test for fit. On top, frame for the sink and test that the sink will fit. Frame the countertop so that the backerboard will be supported at least every 12 inches or so.

4 Frame the Dining Counter

The dining counter must overhang about 15 inches to make

room for diners' legs. Build a double 2-by-4 wall. Construct a counter frame out of 2 by 4s and firmly anchor the frame to the double wall using angle irons and screws. The counter should feel firm when you push down on it at the outside corner.

5 Apply Backerboard and Stucco

Cut pieces of concrete backerboard to fit the framed counter and then apply them over both the sides and the top. Attach the backerboard to the wood studs with backerboard screws. Adhere the backerboard to the concrete block using thinset mortar. As you work, test again to make sure that the doors, sink, and grill will fit. Apply two coats of stucco to all the visible sides of the counter (see pages 126–127). Either apply stucco with integral color or apply paint after the stucco has dried completely.

6 Tile the Top

Apply waterproof tile backing to cover both countertops. Cut the backing with a utility knife and use thinset mortar to hold it in place. See pages 132–135 for instructions on applying tiles. Lay the tiles in a dry run, making sure you will not end up with narrow slivers. Once you are satisfied with the layout, set the tiles in latex- or polymer-reinforced thinset mortar. Once the mortar has set, apply grout and wipe clean.

7 Install the Doors, Grill, and Sink

Hook up the plumbing for the sink (see pages 144–147), and the gas line or propane tank for the grill (see pages 140–141). Set and attach the doors and the grill (see pages 148–149). Apply caulk to the door flanges and the sink flanges as you set them in to make them watertight. Plug in the refrigerator.

This long counter sitting demurely against the fence actually packs quite a punch. Fully equipped with modern amenities, it also boasts a decorative concrete countertop with glass tiles (inset). *DESIGN: RANSOHOFF, BLANCHFIELD, JONES, INC. LANDSCAPE ARCHITECTS*

full of surprises

This outdoor kitchen is attractive and useful without calling undue attention to itself. The beige-stuccoed counter walls and the earth-toned concrete countertop blend into a natural setting. The attached low walls on each side add to the sense that the counter is a part of its surroundings. The overhead is made of natural redwood that is only lightly stained, and a trellis encourages plants to climb up and around.

Take a closer look, however, and you will see some stunning effects. The overhead features some very impressive joinery, as well as decorative corbels and overhead lighting. The ample concrete counter is tinted a lovely dark shade with speckles of white, and it is flecked with small glass tiles that have been carefully embedded. The stainless-steel grill, side burner, warming drawer, and refrigerator make this a great place for preparing food.

THE DESIGN

The counter is a simple rectangle 12 feet long, which makes for plenty of countertop space. As the illustration on the opposite page shows, a large unit like this allows plenty of space for the appliances, so you have room to build almost entirely with full-or half-sized blocks. Here, the 6-inch blocks were reinforced with vertical rebar and the cells were filled with concrete, but in your area this may not be necessary.

To the right of the counter, a short wall encloses a planting area. To the left, there is a shelf at the same height where you could place an appliance or a large flowerpot.

GETTING READY

Check local codes to find out how thick the concrete footing will need to be. (To build a lighter unit using steel or wood studs, see pages 122–125.) Purchase cooking units and doors ahead of time so you can test while you build to make sure they will fit. Plan how you will run the conduit for the electrical lines (see pages 108–109). Plan to run gas pipe unless you will use a propane tank instead.

A concrete countertop is an ambitious project. If you want a very smooth and finished-looking top, hire a pro. To build a casual-looking top, see pages 136–139.

TO SUPPORT THE GRILL, SEE PAGES 106–107

MATERIALS LIST

FOR THE COUNTER:
- Grill
- Side burner
- Outdoor cabinet door
- Refrigerator
- Gas pipe, shutoff valves, and connections
- Electrical supplies: cable or conduit with wire, boxes, GFCI receptacles
- Concrete for the footing
- 6" × 8" × 16" Concrete block
- Steel reinforcing bar
- Mortar mix
- 3" angle irons
- Stucco mix
- 2 × 4s and 2 × 2s to build forms for the countertop

- ½" concrete backerboard
- Concrete and reinforcing bar for the countertop
- Decorative glass tiles to embed in the countertop
- Silicone caulk
- Acrylic masonry sealer

FOR THE OVERHEAD:
- 6 × 6s for posts
- Concrete for the postholes
- 2 ×10s for the beams
- 1 × 8s trim
- 2 × 2s for trim and the trellis
- 2 × 4s for the trellis
- 4 × 10s for beams and corbels
- 4 × 8s for rafters
- 3 × 4s for top pieces
- Deck screws: 6", 3", 2½"

THE SUBSTRUCTURE

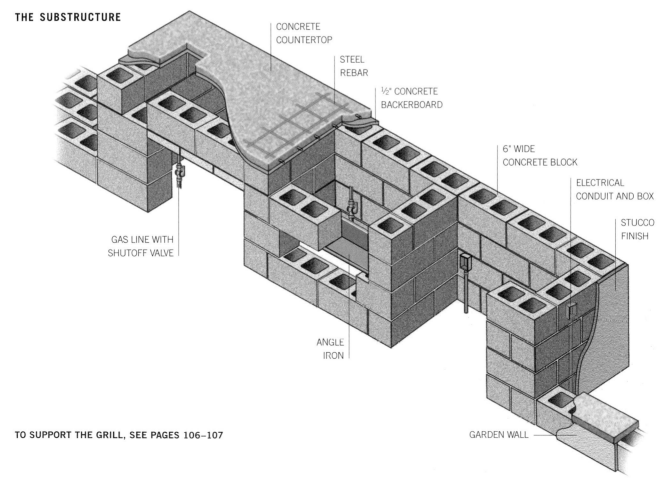

CONCRETE COUNTERTOP

STEEL REBAR

½" CONCRETE BACKERBOARD

6" WIDE CONCRETE BLOCK

ELECTRICAL CONDUIT AND BOX

STUCCO FINISH

GAS LINE WITH SHUTOFF VALVE

ANGLE IRON

GARDEN WALL

If you want to embed small tiles or other decorative elements, choose the pieces carefully and plan for their placement ahead of time.

In this project, local building codes would not permit a full-blown overhead structure. So this overhead has only 4 feet of shade elements, which allowed it to be considered officially a "fence." If you want more shade, you will probably need to install posts and beams in a rectangle rather than in a row. The joinery techniques are difficult to make with 4-by lumber, but it is much easier to make similar joints with 2-by overhead pieces (in which case 4-by-4 posts will look more to scale than 6 by 6s).

THE COUNTER

1 Run Lines and Pour a Footing

Dig a hole for the concrete footing and build forms at the same height as or slightly higher than the surrounding patio. Run the gas and electrical lines through trenches and into the excavation, making sure they will poke up in convenient locations. You will need two gas supplies, one for the burner and one for the grill; and at least two electrical receptacles, one on the side of the unit and one inside, for the refrigerator.

Strengthen the slab by running steel reinforcing bars through the footing in a grid pattern. If you will fill the block cells with concrete, also place reinforcing bars vertically so they will run up through every other block cell. Pour and finish the footing (see pages 110–111).

2 Build the Walls

After the concrete has cured for a few days, construct the block walls (see pages 114–117). Set reinforcing wire every other course. Use angle irons to support the blocks that span the doorways. Check to be sure that the doors and appliances will fit. Fill the cells with concrete if that is required. Run electrical conduit and install the boxes. Install the inside electrical receptacle (see pages 142–143).

3 Frame and Pour the Countertop

See pages 136–139 for instructions on making a decorative concrete countertop. Cut pieces of concrete backerboard to fit,

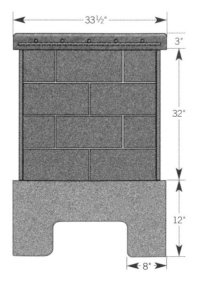

SIDE VIEW

- 33½"
- 3"
- 32"
- 12"
- 8"

set them in place, and make sure the grill and burner will fit in the openings. Inside the counter, prop boards to support the backerboard while you pour. Construct a form for the concrete using 2 by 4s and 2 by 2s. Add reinforcing mesh or a grid of rebar that will run through the center of the countertop's thickness. Mix a batch of colored concrete and pour it into the form. Trowel the surface smooth. Remove the form boards and trowel the edges as well. Once the top is smoothed to your liking, carefully press the small tiles so they are flush with the counter surface. Allow the concrete to cure slowly, then wipe the tiles clean once the concrete is completely dry. Then apply a coat or two of acrylic sealer.

4 Stucco

Use painter's tape and plastic to protect the concrete top from stucco splatters. Apply two or three coats of stucco to all the visible sides of the counter (see pages 126–127). Either apply a finish coat of stucco with integral color, or paint the stucco after it has dried. Install the outside electrical receptacles.

5 Install the Appliances and Doors

Hook up flexible lines for the cooking units. Set and install the grill and the side burner (see pages 148–149). Attach the doors and plug in the refrigerator.

THE OVERHEAD

1 Set the Posts

See pages 150–153 for general instructions on planning and installing an overhead. In the structure shown on page 60, there are four 6-by-6 posts and two intervening 4-by-4 posts to support the trellis only. Dig post-holes, set the posts in the holes, check to be sure they are lined up, and temporarily brace them. Cut the posts to height.

2 Make the Corbels

These pieces are mostly decorative, but they also provide some support for the rafters. Cut the corbels following the pattern shown at right, or come up with a design of your own. If you are making them out of 4 by 8, you will need a band saw to make the curved cuts. If you are using 2 by 8 instead, a high-quality jigsaw will do the job.

3 Assemble the Beam and Corbels

Cut the beam to overhang the posts by about a foot on either side. Make decorative cuts on the ends to match the corbels. Also cut the rafters to size, with decorative cuts at each end. Cut notches in the bottom of the beam where each corbel will go. Four corbels go on top of the posts, and two are evenly spaced in the middle. Fit the corbels into the beam, then drill a pilot hole and drive a screw to attach each one.

4 Assemble the Shade Section

With a helper or two, lift the beam with corbels onto the tops of the posts. Drill angled pilot holes and drive screws to attach the beam to the posts. Set the rafters on top of the corbels and attach them in the same way. Cut 3-by-4 top pieces to length so they overhang the rafters by about 8 inches on each side, then attach them with screws.

5 Build the Trellis

The illustration below shows the trellis from behind. First use 3-inch screws to attach a horizontal 2 by 2, running the length of the trellis, at the desired height. Place a 2 by 4 on top of the 2 by 2 and attach it to the back of the posts by driving 6-inch screws. Mark the posts for evenly spaced horizontal 2 by 2s and attach them to the posts. Mark the horizontals for evenly spaced vertical 2 by 2s. Cut the verticals to length and attach them to the horizontals using 2½-inch screws.

CORBEL PATTERN

OVERHEAD ASSEMBLY

TRELLIS FROM BEHIND

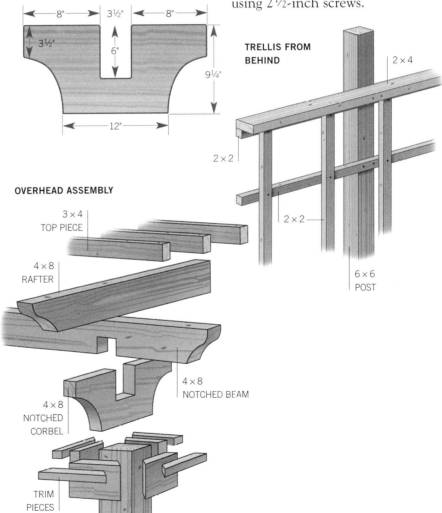

2 × 4

2 × 2

2 × 2

6 × 6 POST

3 × 4 TOP PIECE

4 × 8 RAFTER

4 × 8 NOTCHED BEAM

4 × 8 NOTCHED CORBEL

TRIM PIECES

6 × 6 POST

covered brick kitchen

This home's backyard is subject to heavy winds and intense sunlight, so the owners opted for a sheltered outdoor kitchen. With a solid roof and walls on three sides, it is a comfortable place to be regardless of the weather. But it still has a pleasant outdoorsy feel, since it is open to the backyard on one side. Overhead skylights and large windows add to the sense of openness. The overall effect is a bit like an old-fashioned covered porch, but with modern cooking facilities. The cabinet doors and the refrigerator panel were all painted the same color for a unified look. The owners did not want stainless steel to be a prominent visual element, so they reused an older gas grill that sits nearly flush with the countertop surface.

THE DESIGN

The counter is a double-wythe wall, meaning it is built two bricks thick. Bricks rise up at the rear to form the backsplash. The countertop is mostly covered with 6-inch ceramic tile, but the outer edges are made of brick. A concrete slab forms the substrate for the tiles. This counter is not as heavy as one made of concrete block, but it should be supported by a reinforced concrete slab.

Because the counter is sheltered, indoor-style wood cabinetry

is practical. The cabinet doors open to reveal spacious, long drawers that slide smoothly on heavy-duty glides, making it easy to reach stored dishes and utensils. The cabinets were custom made, but similar factory-made units could easily be incorporated into a counter like this.

The countertop substrate is a steel-reinforced concrete slab. You could use two layers of concrete backerboard instead. Because the tiles butt into, and are flush with, bricks at the perimeter, there is no need for bullnose or V-cap pieces at the edges.

GETTING READY

Building brick walls calls for good masonry skills. See pages 118–121 for instructions. If you do not have experience, you may choose to hire a pro. Check local codes to find out how thick a concrete footing you need.

Plan how you will run the gas and electrical lines, as well as the drain and water supply pipes. You may also want to run low-voltage wiring for the lights in the back-splash. Buy the grill, cooktop, sink, refrigerator, and cabinets ahead of time. Have them on hand as you build so you can be sure everything will fit.

The outdoor kitchen shown uses common brick, which has a pleasant rustic appearance. You may choose among a wide variety of face bricks, which have more finished-looking surfaces. Builders often use face brick on parts that will show and common brick for parts that will be hidden.

Above: This spacious, sheltered cooking area has all the amenities of an indoor kitchen, yet retains an inviting outdoorsy feel because it is open to the yard on one side and has skylights above. *Right:* Several generously sized sliding drawers keep supplies handy. DESIGN: JANET BELL, JANET BELL & ASSOCIATES

1 Excavate and Run Utility Lines

Dig a hole for the concrete footing. Run the gas, plumbing, and electrical lines through it, and make sure they will poke up at convenient locations (see pages 108–109). If the sink is near a hot-water line, you may choose to run a separate hot-water pipe. Otherwise run only a cold-water line and install an on-demand water heater inside the counter (see page 144). For drainage, you may be able to tie into a drain line in the house.

2 Form and Pour the Footing

Using 2 by 4s, construct a form for the slab at the same height as or slightly higher than the surrounding patio. Strengthen the footing by running reinforcing bars horizontally through the footing in a grid pattern every 12 inches or as required by local codes. Pour and finish the footing (see pages 110–111).

3 Build the Counter

After the concrete has cured for a few days, construct the brick walls (see pages 118–121). Use a chalk line and a dry run of bricks to lay out for the bottom rows. Mix and throw a line of mortar on the slab, then build leads at the corners. Use line blocks to stretch mason's line, which will guide you in the placement of the interior bricks.

The project shown uses a "running bond" brick pattern, which does not include bond bricks that tie the two wythes together. If you use this pattern, lay corrugated metal wall ties across the two wythes every few bricks. Tool the mortar joints as you go.

MATERIALS LIST

- Grill
- Two-burner cooktop
- Custom-made cabinet unit with doors and drawers
- Gas pipe, shutoff valve, and connections
- Concrete and reinforcing bar for the footing
- Mortar mix
- Common brick
- 3" angle irons
- Sand-mix concrete for the countertop substrate
- Plywood and 2 × 4s for concrete forms
- Sink with faucet
- Plumbing supplies: drain lines, supply lines, stop valves
- Electrical supplies: cable or conduit with wire, boxes, GFCI receptacles
- Refrigerator
- Low-voltage lights
- Countertop tile
- Thinset mortar
- Grout
- Silicone caulk
- Acrylic masonry sealer

When you reach an opening for a door or the refrigerator, use two angle irons to support the bricks above the lintels. Build the front and side wythes to the full height of the countertop, and build the interior wythes one brick short of full height. (The concrete substrate for the tiles will rest on this interior wythe.) On the rear walls, build up the backsplashes.

4 Pour the Countertop Substrate

For instructions on forming and finishing a concrete substrate, see pages 136–139, though the techniques differ here. Allow the mortar to cure for a few days, then build a form for the concrete substrate. Cut pieces of plywood to fit snugly between the walls. The plywood will temporarily support the concrete substrate. Prop the plywood in place with 2-by-4 framing. The plywood should feel firm at all points, and there should be no gap larger than $\frac{1}{4}$ inch through which wet concrete could leak. Build 2-by-4 forms for the areas where the cooktop, grill, and sink will go. Check that appliances will fit.

Cut pieces of reinforcing bar and tie them together with wire to form a grid running through the formed area. Pour and finish the concrete. Wait several days before removing the framing and plywood.

5 Set the Tiles

Lay countertop tiles following the methods shown on pages 132–135. Make the cuts and set all the tiles in a dry run, then lay one section at a time in thinset mortar. Tap with a beater board from time to time to ensure an even surface. Wait a day for the mortar to harden. Apply acrylic sealer to the top bricks so they will not be stained by the grout. Apply grout and wipe clean.

6 Install the Appliances

Run electrical lines and hook up the plumbing as shown on pages 142–147. Attach the faucet and trap to the sink, set the sink, and make the plumbing connections. Install a gas shutoff valve and flexible line for both the burner and the grill. Install the cabinet doors. After a week or so, apply a coat of acrylic sealer to the tile, grout, and bricks.

THE SUBSTRUCTURE

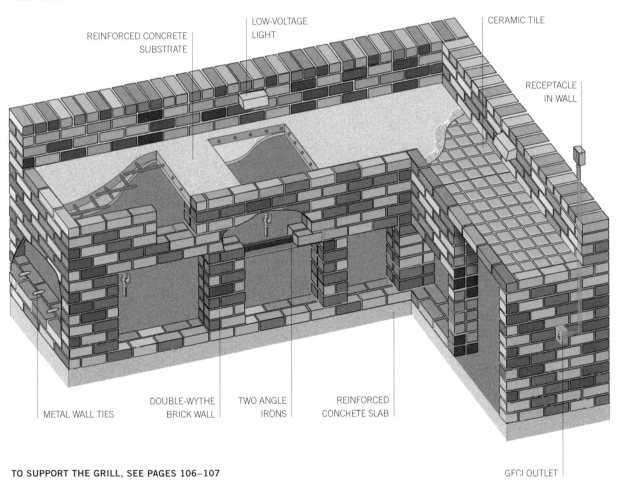

REINFORCED CONCRETE SUBSTRATE

LOW-VOLTAGE LIGHT

CERAMIC TILE

RECEPTACLE IN WALL

METAL WALL TIES

DOUBLE-WYTHE BRICK WALL

TWO ANGLE IRONS

REINFORCED CONCRETE SLAB

GFCI OUTLET

TO SUPPORT THE GRILL, SEE PAGES 106–107

wood cabinets in a niche

Tucked away in a walled corner and roofed with a vine-covered cedar overhead, this is a comfortable and secluded setting. The wood tones of the cabinets and the overhead, combined with the intimate foliage, give this outdoor kitchen a woodsy feel. An almost white cast concrete countertop works well with the antiqued concrete wall. The modest kitchen is equipped with a sink, a large grill, and receptacles for small appliances and a refrigerator, which can fit inside the cabinet.

This cozy kitchen decorated with Mediterranean touches sits beneath a leafy overhead which provides shade and seclusion. DESIGN: PEDERSEN ASSOCIATES, LANDSCAPE ARCHITECTS

THE DESIGN

Wood is an unusual finish material for outdoor kitchens. But if you live in a dry climate, it can be practical. Mahogany was chosen for this project for its beauty and its resistance to rot and warping. The extra cost of mahogany is not significant in this case, as so little is needed. Seal the wood with two or more coats of finish or paint, and recoat it every year or so. Direct sunlight can be just as damaging as rain, so provide shade. Also check grill manufacturer recommendations to be sure wood surfaces are protected from the heat of the grill.

This kitchen is nestled between a storage shed and two walls. To make room for foot traffic, the overhead has one supporting bracket attached to the shed and another attached to a post that is offset from the corner of the wall.

GETTING READY

You might chose to purchase ready-made cabinets rather than build them yourself, but chances are they will not be weather-resistant. Also, it may be impossible to buy a stock cabinet that is the right height for under the grill.

Building cabinets with doors calls for woodworking skills and a good assortment of tools, including a table saw or a radial-arm saw. The alternative shown here is to build the frame yourself and then hire a cabinet shop to make the doors for you.

Coordinate the building of the overhead with the construction of the counter. It may be simplest to build the counter first and then add the overhead. Or you may set the overhead's posts, build the counter, and then finish the overhead.

A wood counter with a thin concrete top is not very heavy,

THE SUBSTRUCTURE

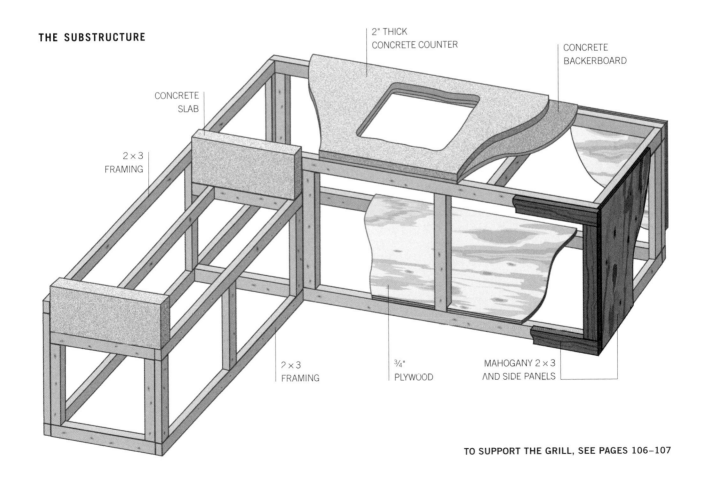

2" THICK CONCRETE COUNTER

CONCRETE BACKERBOARD

CONCRETE SLAB

2 × 3 FRAMING

2 × 3 FRAMING

¾" PLYWOOD

MAHOGANY 2 × 3 AND SIDE PANELS

TO SUPPORT THE GRILL, SEE PAGES 106–107

so it does not need a thick concrete footing. However, it should rest on a solid and level surface.

Purchase a grill with a heat jacket that protects abutting wood surfaces from overheating.

MATERIALS LIST

FOR THE COUNTER:
- Grill
- Sink with faucet and trap
- Gas pipe, shutoff valve, and connections
- Plumbing supplies: drain lines, supply lines, stop valves
- Electrical supplies: cable or conduit with wire, boxes, GFCI receptacles
- 2 × 3s, mahogany or another rot-resistant lumber
- Deck screws: 2½", 2"
- Pressure-treated plywood
- Cabinet doors from a wood shop
- Hinges and knobs or pulls
- Stain and sealer

CONCRETE COUNTERTOP
- See pages 136–139

FOR THE OVERHEAD:
- 6 × 6s for posts
- Concrete for the postholes
- 4 × 6s for beams
- 2 × 2s for top pieces
- 9" lag screws with washers
- Deck screws: 3", 1"

THE COUNTER

1 Run the Utility Lines

If the counter abuts the indoor kitchen, it may be relatively easy to hook up the utility lines directly through the wall. Otherwise, you will need to run lines through trenches. Run wiring for the receptacles, grill, and instant water heater, and install the rough plumbing (see pages 108–109).

2 Build the Frames

Construct counter frames out of lumber that is strong but finished-looking. Here, mahogany 2 by 3s were used. Be sure to choose lumber that is straight and free of twists. The frame should be 34½ inches high and about 24 inches deep. (The countertop is 1½ inches thick and overhangs the frame by 1 inch.)

First, build the long counter, the one with the sink. Cut the front and rear horizontal pieces to length, then the verticals. Working on a large, flat surface, assemble the frames. Position the vertical pieces where the doors will be. Attach the pieces by drilling pilot holes and driving two deck screws at each joint. Use a framing square to check each joint before you fasten it. (If you have the tools and skills, make dowel or mortise-and-tenon joints instead.) Build the side frames in the same way and attach them to the insides of the front and rear frames. On the back of the frame and the side that does not show, cut pieces of ¾-inch pressure-treated plywood to fit and then attach the pieces with screws.

Set the long counter frame in place, check it for square, and anchor it to any abutting walls by driving deck screws. Cut two or three top braces to fit, space them evenly, and attach them with deck screws. Construct the shorter frame in the same way. However, the front of this frame must be lower to support the grill. Follow the manufacturer's framing instructions so that the grill ends up at the desired height. Set the shorter frame in place, check it for square, and screw it to the longer frame.

Once the frames are in place, cut pieces of ¾-inch plywood for the floor and screw them in place. Install the finish electrical, gas, and plumbing (see pages 140–147). Measure the door openings and have a cabinetmaker produce doors to fit the openings. Screw self-closing hinges onto the doors, then position the doors and screw the hinges into the frame. Add the door pulls of your choice.

3 Make the Counter

The wood frames could be covered with backerboard and tile (see pages 132–135), but this countertop is made of cast concrete. See pages 136–139 for basic instructions on casting a concrete countertop. In addition to the large countertop slabs, cast two pieces to rest on end at each side of the grill.

THE OVERHEAD

1 Set the Posts

See pages 150–153 for general instructions on building an overhead. In this design, two brackets—one attached to the shed and one to a post—take the place of one post. Decorative brackets extend out to support the beams where there are no posts.

Use layout lines to determine the positions of the posts. Dig postholes at least 2 feet deep. Set a 6-by-6 post in each hole and brace them temporarily. Pour concrete or well-tamped soil into the holes now, or wait until the overhead is finished and pour then. Cut the front and rear posts to the same height and the side posts $1\frac{1}{2}$ inches shorter.

2 Make the Brackets

Have a lumberyard use a band saw to cut the brackets out of 4-by-12 lumber, following the pattern shown at right. Alternatively, make simple straight brackets by cutting the ends of a 4 by 6 at 45 degrees.

3 Install the Front and Rear Beams

Cut the front and rear 4 by 6s to length. Make a light pencil mark on the front beam where it will rest on the post. Working with two helpers and some sturdy ladders, raise the front beam into position on top of the post. Use a piece of lumber to temporarily prop the unsupported end so that it is level, and have the helpers hold the beam in place while you install the bracket. Hold the bracket in place, drill pilot holes, and then drive lag screws with washers to secure the brackets. Attach the beam to the post by angle-drilling pilot holes and driving deck screws. The rear beam rests on two posts. These beams will not be stable until you install the rest of the pieces, so take care not to bump them as you work.

4 The Side Beams

Cut the side beams to length, 12 inches longer than the distance they will span from the front to the rear beam. Use a reciprocating saw to cut a decorative pattern at each end. Working with two helpers, raise a side beam into position. At each corner, the side beam should run 8 inches past the front or rear beam, and its top should be $1\frac{1}{2}$ inches lower than the front or rear beam. Use a framing square to check each corner, then drill pilot holes and drive two 9-inch lag screws into each joint.

5 Add the Top Pieces

Cut a number of 2-by-2 top pieces so they overhang the beams by 4 inches on each side. The lower pieces rest on the side beams, and the upper ones rest on the front and rear beams. Space the top pieces so as to achieve the amount of shade you desire, and attach them to the beams by drilling pilot holes and driving $2\frac{1}{2}$-inch deck screws. Also drive screws to attach the 2 by 2s to each other.

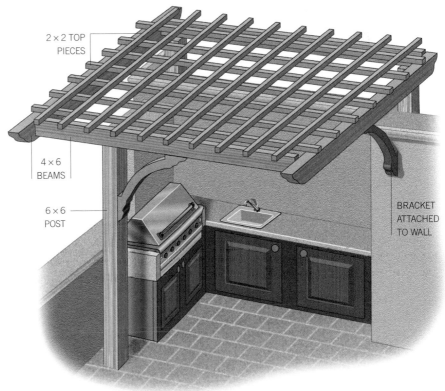

2 × 2 TOP PIECES

4 × 6 BEAMS

6 × 6 POST

BRACKET ATTACHED TO WALL

tuscan setting

Terra-cotta hues set a mellow mood in this outdoor kitchen that is reminiscent of an Italian villa. Brown and beige tones reflect light with less intensity than white tones, so they are easy on the eye. They also do not absorb and radiate the sun's heat the way darker colors would.

The kitchen includes a pizza oven, a large gas grill, and a refrigerator. Instead of installing a sink with a faucet, the owners chose a simple but practical arrangement: two spigots attached to adjacent posts, about 2 feet above the countertop—just the right height for filling large pots.

A few artistic touches complete the picture. Decorative tiles set into the stucco surface of the counter complement the tiles that cover the upper portion of the pizza oven. A pair of custom-made copper doors below the oven keep the wood logs hidden and protected. The oven's roof is also copper, which will turn a lovely verdigris hue in a few years. A small copper butterfly near the refrigerator and a long pizza paddle hung near the oven's hearth serve as finishing touches.

A long simple layout lends a feeling of wide open space, while artfully placed tiles and other small decorative touches add charm.
DESIGN: RANSOHOFF, BLANCHFIELD, JONES, INC. LANDSCAPE ARCHITECTS

THE DESIGN

The 14-foot-long counter provides plenty of work and storage space. The walls are made of 6-inch concrete block capped with 2-inch block. This gives the walls a total height of 34 inches, so the countertop is a standard 36 inches high once the 2-inch-thick granite slab is added. The walls are covered with stucco, and a polished granite slab forms the countertop. Stainless-steel doors provide access to storage space inside the counter. The large gas grill includes an integrated two-burner cooktop.

The pizza oven is perpendicular to the counter. The oven is housed in a structure made of concrete block and a raised concrete slab. For instructions on building an oven like this, see pages 76–79. The oven is topped with a copper roof.

GETTING READY

You will likely hire pros to install the pizza oven and the granite slab, but you may choose to build and stucco the counter yourself. Buy the grill, refrigerator, and doors and have them on hand as you build so you can be sure everything will fit. Contact a granite countertop supplier to get an idea of the price and how long it will take to have the countertop delivered. The supplier will take final measurements after the counter is built. Also contact a sheet-metal shop about ordering

---

MATERIALS LIST

FOR THE COUNTER:
- Grill with side burner
- Outdoor cabinet doors
- Refrigerator
- Gas pipe, shutoff valve, and connections
- Electrical supplies: cable or conduit with wire, boxes, GFCI receptacles
- Water supply pipe, fittings, and spigots
- Concrete for the footing
- 6" × 8" × 16" Concrete block
- Mortar mix
- ½" reinforcing bar
- Decorative tiles
- Stucco mix
- Granite countertop
- Silicone caulk

FOR THE PIZZA OVEN:
- Materials as listed on page 76
- Ceramic tiles
- Custom copper door
- Copper roof and chimney

---

a custom copper door. Again, the final measurements will be made after the oven is built.

1 Excavate and Run the Lines, and Pour the Footing

Excavate for a footing and slab that will support the counter and the oven and that meet local building codes (see pages 108–111). Run the plumbing line for the spigots, the electrical line, and the gas line (unless you will use a propane tank). Build forms for the slab and add a grid of rebar. Pour and finish the concrete.

---

2 Build the Counter

After the concrete has cured for a few days, construct block walls (see pages 114–117). As you build, place vertical reinforcing bars through some of the cells and fill those cells with concrete. Also place ladder-type reinforcing wire every other course. Use angle irons to support the blocks that span the doorways. From time to time, check to be sure that the doors, refrigerator, and grill will fit. Run any electrical lines through the blocks as needed.

3 Build the Pizza Oven

See pages 76–79 for instructions on building the housing, assembling the oven, adding insulation, assembling the chimney, tiling the surround and hearth, and building a roof for the pizza oven.

4 Tile and Stucco the Counter

Attach decorative tiles so they will be flush with the stucco that will surround them. The total thickness of the stucco will be about 1⅛ inches, so you will likely need to cut a strip of concrete backerboard the same size as the tiles and apply it to the block with thinset mortar, then apply the tiles on top of the backerboard. You may need to apply extra-thick layers of thinset mortar in order to have the tiles stick out the correct distance. Cover the tiles with masking tape to protect them while you apply the stucco.

Apply the first coat of stucco and allow it to cure for a few days. Then apply the second coat and create the finish texture of your choice (see pages 126–127). You may choose to tint the finish coat or apply paint later.

5 Have the Granite Countertop Installed

Once the counter is built, have the granite company come out and measure for the countertop. Depending on how busy the company is, you may have to wait several weeks for installation. Discuss how you want the edges

to be finished. In this case, they were simply rounded. For a different treatment that makes the slab appear to be 4 inches thick, see pages 43–44. Granite is impervious to most stains, but you might want to apply a sealer anyway for extra protection.

6 Install the Appliances and Door

Hook up the grill to the gas line. Apply silicone caulk to seal the appliances and install them in the openings (see pages 148–149). Apply caulk to the doors and install them as well. Plug in the refrigerator.

THE SUBSTRUCTURE

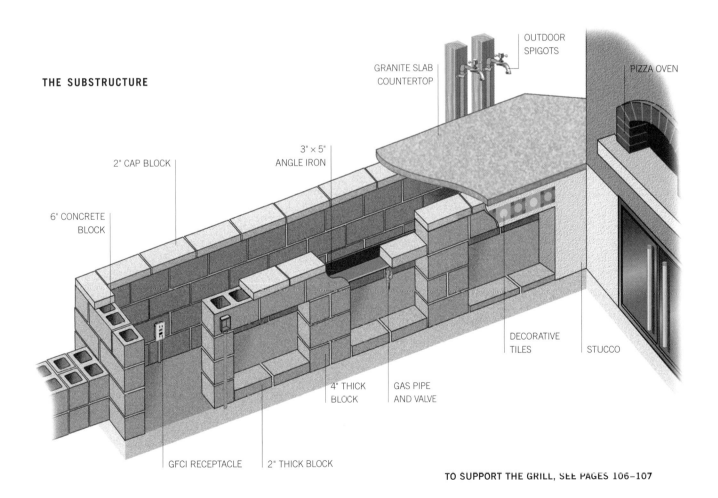

OUTDOOR SPIGOTS

GRANITE SLAB COUNTERTOP

PIZZA OVEN

2" CAP BLOCK

3" × 5" ANGLE IRON

6" CONCRETE BLOCK

DECORATIVE TILES

STUCCO

4" THICK BLOCK

GAS PIPE AND VALVE

GFCI RECEPTACLE

2" THICK BLOCK

TO SUPPORT THE GRILL, SEE PAGES 106–107

pizza oven

An Italian-style pizza oven may be the ultimate in outdoor cooking. See pages 16–17 for some of its culinary possibilities. Purchased as a kit, the oven itself must be housed in a sturdy masonry structure. The structure may be covered with stone, tile, or stucco, and the roof may be made of clay tile or sheet metal.

THE DESIGN

A pizza oven is typically attached to a counter, but these pages focus on it as a separate project, since building one is a challenging job. The oven may be made of a special terra-cotta Italian clay, but the oven shown here is made of refractory concrete, which is somewhat less expensive yet has essentially the same cooking properties. The clay or concrete is porous, so it can absorb steam and produce breads with crisp crusts. The roof and sides of the oven are curved to allow heat to circulate freely. The flue and chimney are positioned just behind the door to remove smoke efficiently and to allow the food to be seen easily.

In the usual outdoor arrangement (these ovens can be installed indoors as well if they are properly vented), the oven is placed at a comfortable height—about 48 inches off the ground—and the space below is used to store firewood.

GETTING READY

This is a serious building project requiring a significant budget—the oven alone runs over $2,000. Both the footing and the raised slab must be strengthened with reinforcing metal. It can be accomplished by a person with good masonry skills and patient attention to detail, but in most cases people hire pros for a structure like this.

Locate the pizza oven well away from any structures or trees, which could inhibit the chimney's draw. Purchase the oven, read the installation instructions, and plan a structure that will adequately support and house the oven.

Form and pour a reinforced concrete slab that meets local building codes (see pages 110–111).

MATERIALS LIST

- Pizza oven kit, complete with door and flue
- Oven thermometer
- Chimney pipe and smoke arrester
- Concrete and rebar for the footing and the slab
- Masonry screws
- Lumber and plywood for forming the slab
- 8" concrete blocks
- Concrete blocks for building around the chimney
- Mortar
- Refractory mortar
- Mineral wool or vermiculite board
- Vermiculite and sand for insulating the oven
- Stucco
- Spanish roof tiles
- Polished granite pieces for the surround and corners
- Outdoor lights

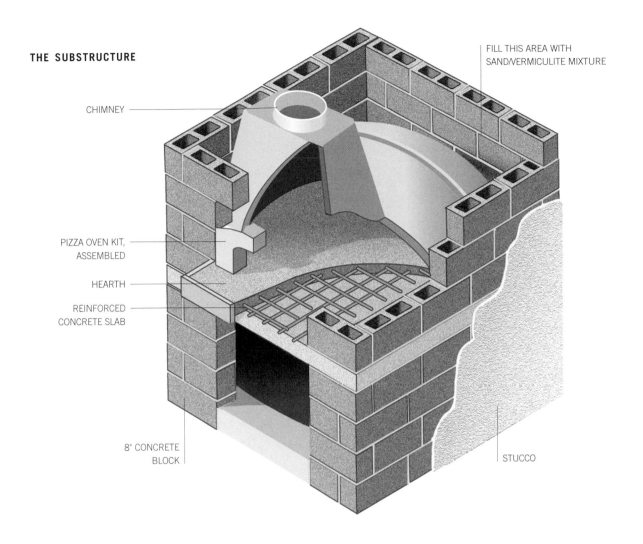

CHIMNEY

FILL THIS AREA WITH
SAND/VERMICULITE MIXTURE

PIZZA OVEN KIT,
ASSEMBLED

HEARTH

REINFORCED
CONCRETE SLAB

8" CONCRETE
BLOCK

STUCCO

1 **Build Support for the Raised Slab**
The structure may stand alone, or it may be attached to a kitchen counter. Build concrete block walls (see pages 114–117) to the desired height of the oven floor. Long pieces of vertical rebar should run through every other cell of the blocks. To support the slab while it is being poured, construct a framework using 2 by 4s. On all sides, support the ledger pieces with masonry screws driven into the blocks. Attach vertical 2 by 4s to support the horizontals in the middle. Bend and run pieces of rebar that span the floor and are inserted into the block cells.

2 Build the Forms

Cut pieces of ¾-inch plywood for the floor and attach them to the supports. The plywood should fit snugly. Cut strips of plywood to form the sides. Attach the sides with screws, then add 2 by 4s to reinforce them. Build a small form for the hearth, which protrudes out of the oven; the hearth is raised to the thickness of the oven's floor. Assemble rebar in a grid that runs through the middle of the slab's thickness. Brush or spray the boards with oil so they don't adhere to the concrete.

3 Pour Concrete and Add the Floor

Pour concrete, taking care to keep the vertical rebar pieces correctly aligned so they will run through the cells of the wall blocks. After the concrete cures, install a layer of mineral wool or vermiculite board to keep the slab from overheating, then set the oven floor on top. Fill any gaps between the bricks with refractory mortar.

4 Assemble the Oven

The oven kit is made of parts that simply stack on top of each other. The pieces are heavy, so you may need to temporarily support one or two pieces with 2 by 4s until the whole unit is assembled.

5 Add the Flue and Build Up

Set the flue portion of the oven in place and seal any gaps with refractory mortar. Build the walls up and fill the cells with a wet concrete mixture. Drill a hole above the oven opening for the thermometer.

6 Build the Chimney and Form Concrete Rafters

Use 2 by 6s and plywood to construct forms for the front and rear rafters. Brace the forms so they are plumb and then pour the concrete. Following the kit manufacturer's instructions, assemble a 6-inch double-wall metal chimney with a spark arrester at the top. Build a block wall around the chimney, leaving vent holes at the top. Drill holes and run wiring for the lights.

7 Frame the Roof and Insulate the Oven

Coat the oven with 3 inches of refractory mortar. Once it dries, fill the cavity around the oven with a mixture of vermiculite and sand. Construct wood framing for the roof.

8 Build the Roof

Attach sheathing to the rafters and install the trim pieces of your choice to the ends and the bottom of the roof. Install tar paper and roofing tiles. Apply mortar to the joints between the tiles and the chimney.

9 Add Finishing Touches

Install the thermometer. Cover the door surround and hearth with granite pieces and apply tiles to the corners. Stucco the walls (see pages 126–127). Install the lights.

winged counter

This counter has enough cooking power to serve a large group, plus it provides space for a few guests to scoot up to the counter and nosh while talking to the cook. Each of its wings is at a 45-degree angle to the center counter, making it easy to reach all areas of the countertop yet also allowing plenty of room for an extra cook or two. The decorative lights make nighttime dining and cooking possible.

THE DESIGN

An island like this is made to sit in the center of a patio rather than up against the house, so it will be prominently on display. This one consists of materials carefully chosen to complement the patio. The faux stones that cover the counter are darker than the patio's flagstones but belong to the same color family. The countertop tiles are darker yet, but their blue-gray color is similarly related.

GETTING READY

Check local codes to find out how thick a concrete footing you need. The counter is built of 6-inch concrete block, with steel reinforcement every 16 inches. (To build with steel studs instead, see pages 122–123.) The countertop cantilevers out 10 inches at the dining area, so a substrate made of concrete backerboard will not be strong enough. You will need to pour a concrete slab for the counter substrate.

An island is by definition separate from the house, so it usually cannot have its drain line tie into the kitchen drain. You will likely need to tie into a sewer line or run into a dry well (see pages 108–109). You will need to run a gas line and a single cold-water supply line into the unit, as well as wiring for two lights and a receptacle. Purchase the sink, appliances, and doors ahead of time so you can build the counter walls and the countertop to fit around them.

1 **Form and Pour the Footing**
Excavate and frame for a concrete footing at the same height as or slightly higher than the surrounding patio. Run gas, plumbing, and electrical lines through it, and make sure they poke up at the most convenient locations. Strengthen the slab by running

THE SUBSTRUCTURE

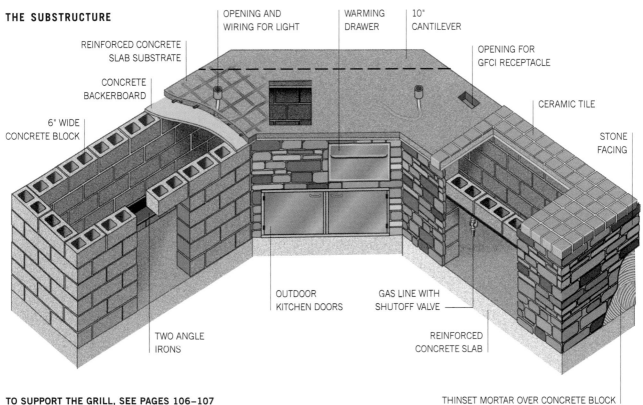

OPENING AND WIRING FOR LIGHT

WARMING DRAWER

10" CANTILEVER

REINFORCED CONCRETE SLAB SUBSTRATE

OPENING FOR GFCI RECEPTACLE

CONCRETE BACKERBOARD

CERAMIC TILE

6" WIDE CONCRETE BLOCK

STONE FACING

TWO ANGLE IRONS

OUTDOOR KITCHEN DOORS

GAS LINE WITH SHUTOFF VALVE

REINFORCED CONCRETE SLAB

TO SUPPORT THE GRILL, SEE PAGES 106–107

THINSET MORTAR OVER CONCRETE BLOCK

steel reinforcing bars horizontally through the footing in a grid pattern every 12 inches, or as required by local codes. You may also run rebar vertically at the corners so they can poke through the blocks later. Pour and finish the footing (see pages 110–111).

2 Build the Walls

After the concrete has cured for a few days, construct the block walls (see pages 114–117). As you build, place vertical reinforcing bars every 16 inches or so, and set reinforcing wire every other course. Use angle irons to support the blocks that span the doorways. From time to time, check to be sure that the doors, sink, and appliances will fit. Fill the cells with concrete if required by code. Before you start on the countertop substrate, add as many utility valves and connections as possible (see pages 140–147).

3 Countertop Substrate

Cut pieces of ½-inch concrete backerboard to fit so that they will overhang the finished counter by 8 inches at the eating side and 2 inches everywhere else. (Be sure to take into account the thickness of the faux stones.) Set the backerboard in mortar on the top of the counter. Check that the sink and grill will fit, and cut holes for the light fixtures and the receptacle. Construct a form out of 2 by 4s anchored against the edges of the backerboard. The top of the form boards

MATERIALS LIST

- Grill
- Warming drawer
- Stainless-steel doors
- Refrigerator
- Sink with faucet and trap
- Instant water heater
- Plumbing supplies: drain lines, supply line, stop valves
- Gas pipe, shutoff valve, and connections
- Electrical supplies: cable or conduit with wire, boxes, GFCI receptacles
- Light fixtures
- Concrete and reinforcing bar for footing
- Concrete block and reinforcing wire
- Angle irons
- Mortar mix
- Faux stone veneer
- Colored mortar for between the stone joints
- Concrete and reinforcing bar for the countertop substrate
- ½" concrete backerboard
- 2 × 4s for concrete forms
- Waterproof tile backing
- Countertop tiles, including bullnose edging and corner pieces
- Fortified grout
- Grout sealer

should be 2 inches higher than the backerboard. Create openings for the light fixtures and the receptacle using plastic pipe or pieces of 1-by lumber. Cut and prop five or six 2 by 4s below the overhanging section to hold it in place during the pour. Install a grid of steel reinforcing bar and pour the slab. Wait several days before removing the props and tiling the top.

4 Cover the Sides

Cut and set faux stones to cover the vertical surfaces (see pages 128–129). Mix a batch of thin-set mortar and apply it with a notched trowel, working in an area that you can cover in 15 minutes or so. Cut the stones carefully around the openings. Fill the joints with mortar as you work. When the mortar is hard enough to retain a thumbprint, tool the joints.

5 Set the Tiles

Lay countertop tiles following the methods shown on pages 132–135. Make the cuts and set all the tiles in a dry run, then lay one section at a time in thinset mortar. Tap with a beater board from time to time to ensure an even surface. At the edges, you may need to hold tiles in place temporarily using pieces of tape. Wait a day or so for the mortar to harden, then apply grout and wipe clean.

6 Install the Appliances

Run electrical lines and hook up the plumbing as shown on pages 142–147. Install the instant water heater. Attach the faucet and trap to the sink, set the sink, and make the plumbing connections from below. Install a gas shutoff valve and flexible line, and set and install the grill. Attach the doors and plug in the refrigerator. After a week or so, apply a coat of sealer to the grout and perhaps to the stones and mortar as well.

adobe oven

If a pizza oven (see pages 76–79) is not in your budget, this is an inexpensive way to get wood-fired taste and baking temperatures of 650–700 degrees. Mud-brick ovens have been used for millennia all around the world. They are still popular in many areas, including Mexico, Italy, France, and the South-western United States. You can build a simple oven yourself, or you may be able to find an arti-san in your area who specializes in one-of-a-kind ovens with designs that range from classic to fanciful.

THE DESIGN

A molded oven is simplicity itself: a mound of clay with a door in front and a vent hole in back. The oven should rest on a fire-safe surface such as a brick patio, but it is not heavy, so no concrete footing is needed. Fire-bricks, simply stacked without mortar, form the base and the lower sides of the oven. The rest is made of molded clay.

GETTING READY

Although ovens can be made of most any mud that contains clay and sand, adobe clay works best. If you live in a Southwestern state, adobe may be the soil beneath your feet when you walk in a desert area. In other regions, you can make your own mix. Combine about 7 parts sand—use

An adobe oven, made of the same earthy clay used for centuries, bakes breads and pizzas and is an inexpensive alternative to a pizza oven. DESIGN: PETER WHITELEY

a mix of both fine and coarse—with 3 parts clay. If clay-rich soil is available in your area, dig up a batch that is nearly free of dark soil and add sand until it feels very rough but still holds its shape when you squeeze it into a ball. To test the proportions of a soil, fill a clear container halfway with water, then fill to the top with some soil. Shake until mixed and then set it down. After an hour or so, you will see large sand and gravel at the bottom, a layer of fine sand in the middle, and clay at the top.

For the mold, you'll need a portion of a cardboard barrel that is about 8 inches in radius. The

MATERIALS LIST

- 14 concrete blocks (8" × 8" × 16")
- 14 concrete cap blocks (8" × 2" × 16")
- 1 cardboard barrel, 28 to 30 gallons
- 1 empty 1-quart can
- 6' square of 6" wire mesh
- 1' of 30"-wide chicken wire
- 4' of rough-sawn redwood 2 × 4
- 2' of redwood 1 × 3
- 1⅝" deck screws
- 3' of 6"-wide aluminum flashing
- 8 large wheelbarrow loads of adobe soil
- 3 bags of portland cement
- 1' square of galvanized wire mesh

custodian at a local school may have one, or call a janitorial supply store.

Find a safe, level location for the oven, at least 5 feet from any combustible surface. Check with local officials about property line setback requirements.

1 Make the Base
Arrange concrete blocks on a flat surface to make a 32-by-54-inch base. Cover the base with an identical layer of cap blocks. Then add a layer of firebricks.

2 Prepare the Barrel
Use a hacksaw or reciprocating saw to cut the barrel in half lengthwise. Be sure to keep the bottom intact. Center an empty quart can on the closed end and trace its outline. Cut the circle so that the can will fit tightly inside.

3 Stack the Sides
Cut two firebricks in half. Starting at the back end of the base, make three U-shaped layers of firebricks to support the half-barrel. Each layer is three bricks long and two bricks wide at the back end. Position the barrel on the bricks, as shown.

4 Attach the Wire Mesh
Cut a 3-by-4-foot piece of the 6-inch wire mesh and shape it so it arcs over the barrel by about 1 inch. Bend and tuck any excess under the bricks at the side. Then cover the mesh with at least one

layer of chicken wire, bending and folding the edges over the rear and open end of the barrel in a similar manner.

5 Make the Door
Cut three 14-inch-long pieces of redwood 2 by 4. Join them together by drilling pilot holes and driving screws through two

parallel lengths of 1 by 3 across the front (see illustration, opposite page). Cut the top into an arch that measures 14 inches tall at the peak and conforms to the basic shape of the open barrel end. Shape the handle from an excess piece of 2 by 4 and attach it to the 1 by 3s with screws. Center and tack flashing around the door's perimeter. Now insert the can into the hole cut in the rear of the barrel.

6 Mix the Mud
Combine 3 parts adobe clay with 1 part portland cement, add water, and mix with a hoe or shovel to the consistency of thick oatmeal. See if the mix holds together by squeezing a lump in your hand.

7 Spread the Mud
Put on a pair of heavy-duty rubber gloves. Working from the base up, pack the adobe-cement mixture firmly over and through the layers of mesh. Push hard to make sure there are no air pockets. Pack the mixture around the can, rotating the can to keep it from being trapped. Form the arch for the door by squeezing the mixture into the chicken wire and periodically inserting the door (with flashing attached) to check fit. Continue adding mud until the coat is 4 to 5 inches thick overall. Let it dry slightly, then smooth the surface with a damp sponge and a scrap of lumber.

8 Cure the Adobe

Wiggle the door and can, then cover the oven with damp towels and a plastic tarp. Keep the towels damp and the oven covered for at least a week while the adobe hardens and cures. Remove the flashing from the door. After removing the coverings and allowing the clay to dry, you may choose to paint the oven with latex paint.

9 Fire It Up

Before you build your first fire in the oven, remove the can from the rear vent and cut and fit a piece of ¼-inch wire mesh in the vent to act as a spark arrester. Build a small fire and keep it burning steadily so the adobe warms slowly and any remaining moisture is baked out.

To cook, build a small kindling fire and allow it to burn for about 10 minutes. Then add three or four logs 3 to 4 inches in diameter and about 1½ feet long.

When they start to burn, add six more logs, 4 to 5 inches around, and toss in about 5 pounds of charcoal briquettes. Let the fire burn for about 3 hours, until most of the wood is gone. Scoop the hot ashes into a fireproof metal container partially filled with water. Quickly clean the oven floor with a wet towel tied to a pole. Set an oven thermometer on the floor. The temperature should be around 650 degrees. The oven will now continue to bake for about 4 hours, with slowly falling temperatures.

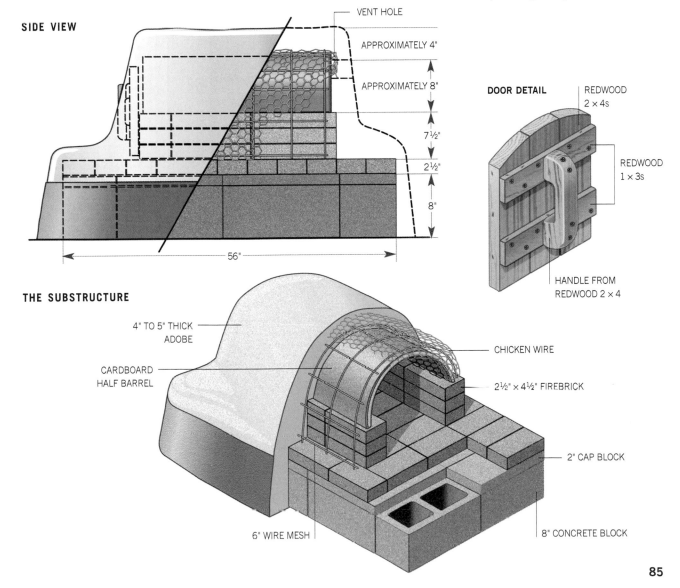

SIDE VIEW

VENT HOLE

APPROXIMATELY 4"

APPROXIMATELY 8"

7½"

2½"

8"

56"

DOOR DETAIL

REDWOOD 2 × 4s

REDWOOD 1 × 3s

HANDLE FROM REDWOOD 2 × 4

THE SUBSTRUCTURE

4" TO 5" THICK ADOBE

CARDBOARD HALF BARREL

CHICKEN WIRE

2½" × 4½" FIREBRICK

2" CAP BLOCK

6" WIRE MESH

8" CONCRETE BLOCK

fire pit with bench

With its venerable stone facing and 16-inch-wide benches around it, this fire pit is a warm and inviting place to sit and chat. The pit is large enough so that people will not get too hot, and the stone surround absorbs and gently radiates warmth. A gas log lighter makes it easy to start a wood fire, or it could be used along with a set of faux ceramic logs. A drain allows the firebox to dry quickly after a rain. You can even cook over the open fire using a rotisserie kit.

This fire pit includes a built-in bench of wide flat stone to comfortably seat a good number of guests in the warmth of a glowing fire. DESIGN: PEDERSEN ASSOCIATES, LANDSCAPE ARCHITECTS

THE SUBSTRUCTURE

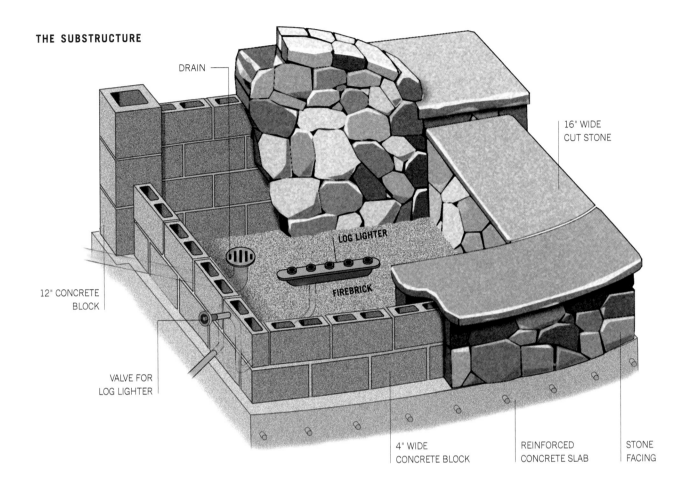

DRAIN

16" WIDE
CUT STONE

LOG LIGHTER

FIREBRICK

12" CONCRETE
BLOCK

VALVE FOR
LOG LIGHTER

4" WIDE
CONCRETE BLOCK

REINFORCED
CONCRETE SLAB

STONE
FACING

THE DESIGN

The structure is supported by a reinforced concrete slab that is 10 inches thick around the perimeter and 6 inches thick in the middle. In an area with freezing winters, local codes may require a deeper footing that extends below the frost line, but most building departments will relax their requirements for a structure this small.

The fire pit is built of steel-reinforced concrete block, which is faced on both sides with natural stone. The walls are made of 4-inch-thick block, while the two pillars are made of 12-inch half block. This stone facing has unmortared joints for a hand-stacked appearance. In an area with freezing winters, it is usually best to mortar joints to keep ice from forming in the joints and damaging the stones. You could also cover this structure with brick, tile, or stucco (see pages 118–121, 130–131, 126–127). If you want to use tile instead, build with 6-inch rather than 4-inch block. The benches and the two pillars are capped with stone slabs that were cut to fit.

GETTING READY

Build in a spot that is at least 5 feet from any combustible surface, such as a fence, an overhead structure, or tree branches. Choose a size and height that are comfortable. Most adults prefer to sit on a bench that is 16 to 17 inches high, but you may choose a different height.

Buy the log lighter before starting construction and keep it nearby for reference as you work. Plan to place the lighter's control at a spot that is convenient but which you can barricade if children are around.

1 Lay Out for the Footing

When laying out for the footing, mark the ground taking into account the thickness of the stones on either side of the blocks; your concrete slab must support the stones. Use stakes and mason's line to mark the square corners and use spray paint for the curved side.

2 Excavate and Form the Footing

Dig a trench around the perimeter, following the layout lines carefully and creating sides that are as vertical as possible. Install wood forms around the excavation. The curve is gentle, so you can probably use 1-by-4 lumber rather than benderboard to form it. Check the forms for level and square. Remove the sod from the interior. Run a grid of string lines across the forms so you can check for depth as you dig the interior. When you reach the bottom of the excavation, scrape rather than bite into the soil.

3 Run the Gas and Drain Lines

You could skip these amenities if you want to build fires from scratch and don't mind mopping the pit after a rain. Otherwise, have a plumber run a gas line into the excavated area and up where it can run through a cell of a block. Install a valve, positioned so it will be on the outside

MATERIALS LIST

- 2" PVC pipe, fittings, and a grate for the drain line
- Gas pipe, fittings, and shutoff valve
- Log lighter
- Concrete for the footing
- Steel reinforcing bar
- Firebricks
- 12" concrete half blocks
- 4" concrete blocks
- Refractory mortar
- Stone facing
- 16"-wide stone slabs cut to fit

of the stone wall. Continue running the gas pipe to the location of the log lighter. Also run 2-inch drainpipe into the area, poking up above the level of the firebricks (see step 6). You will cut this to height later.

4 Pour the Footing

Pound 4-foot-long pieces of steel reinforcing bar perfectly vertically into the ground where they will run through the center of the 12-inch blocks. Also pound in rebar to run through a cell in each of the 4-inch blocks. Local codes may require that you also install steel reinforcing for the footing. Pour the footing and finish it with a magnesium or wood float (see pages 110–111). Allow the footing to cure for at least three days and keep it damp during that time.

5 Build the Walls

Lay the concrete blocks following the instructions on pages 114–117. Where the blocks are laid in a curve, butt their inside corners together and pack mortar into the gaps around the outer face. Check the blocks for level as you work. Cut a hole for the gas pipe using a cold chisel or a drill with a carbide hole saw.

6 Set the Firebricks, Caps, and Stone Facing

Lay the firebrick on the concrete inside the walls, using refractory mortar. Order slabs of stone cut to fit and set them in mortar on the walls and the pillar. Make sure the slabs are level in both directions. Apply stone facing as shown on pages 128–129.

7 Finish

Use a hand saw to cut the drainpipe flush with the top of the firebricks. Install a grate onto the pipe. Though most of the walls are not mortared, you may want to apply a small amount around the gas valve to hold it firmly in place.

chimney smoker

Barbecue purists, especially those who live in the South, will tell you that this is the only way to really barbecue: slow cooking with lots of smoke. This style of cooking is also common in China and elsewhere throughout the world.

Though it does not take up a large space, this smoker will handle up to 10 chickens, roasts, or whole fish at a time. Because it circulates intense, smoky heat around whatever is being cooked, there is no need to turn the food, and you end up with meat that is juicy yet drained of excess fat.

The fire pit supplies the chimney with dense smoke and heat for a southern-style barbeque experience.
DESIGN: IRVINE'S DESIGN, LANDSCAPE ARCHITECTS

THE DESIGN

The heart of the system, the chimney, is a simple cylindrical concrete drainpipe about 2 feet in diameter and 4 feet tall. A square hole cut in the bottom of the drainpipe and positioned next to an adjacent fire pit allows smoke and heat from the fire to enter the chimney. You control the heat by moving the fire nearer to or farther from the chimney's hole and by opening or closing a metal lid atop the chimney.

The chimney and the outer part of the fire pit are made of standard brick. Firebrick is used inside the fire pit. You may choose not to face the chimney with bricks. The chimney could be left plain or be covered with stucco (see pages 126–127).

GETTING READY

The chimney's massive weight must be supported by a thick, reinforced concrete slab. Consult your building department to learn how to pour a slab that will satisfy code requirements.

The brickwork is tricky, so hire a mason if you do not have experience. Because the bricks go around tight curves, they must be bevel cut, as shown on page 92. To make these cuts, rent a wet masonry saw. With practice, you can make precise cuts quickly.

Locate a section of steel-reinforced concrete drainpipe, about 3 inches thick and 22 inches in diameter. A sewer supply source or a salvage yard may sell

THE SUBSTRUCTURE

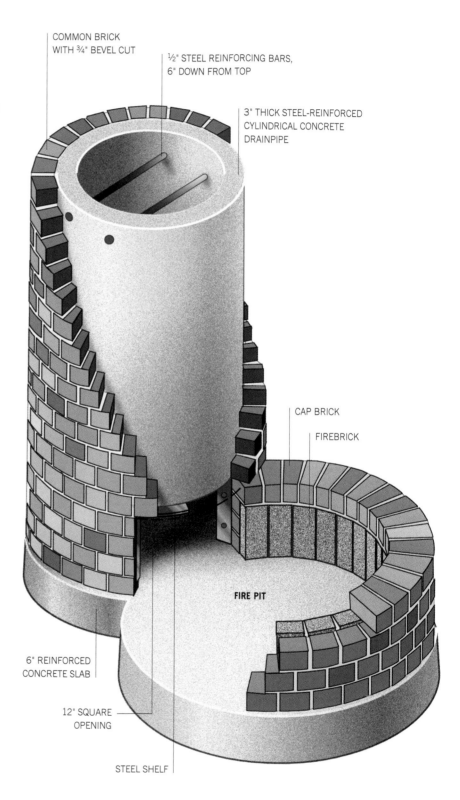

COMMON BRICK WITH ¾" BEVEL CUT

½" STEEL REINFORCING BARS, 6" DOWN FROM TOP

3" THICK STEEL-REINFORCED CYLINDRICAL CONCRETE DRAINPIPE

CAP BRICK

FIREBRICK

FIRE PIT

6" REINFORCED CONCRETE SLAB

12" SQUARE OPENING

STEEL SHELF

SIDE VIEW

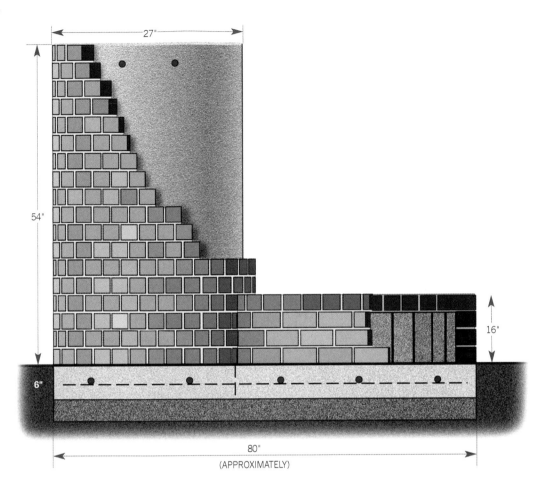

27"

54"

16"

6"

80"
(APPROXIMATELY)

OVERHEAD VIEW

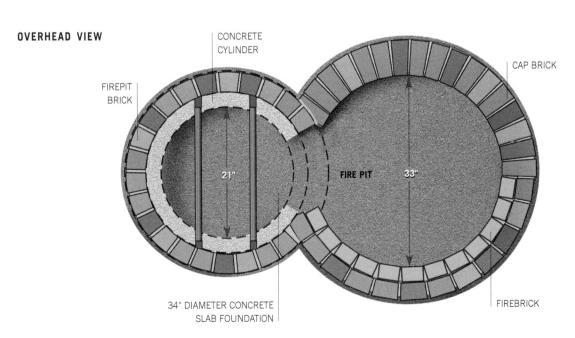

CONCRETE
CYLINDER

CAP BRICK

FIREPIT
BRICK

21"

FIRE PIT

33"

34" DIAMETER CONCRETE
SLAB FOUNDATION

FIREBRICK

you one. If possible, pay the supplier to cut it for you. Otherwise you'll need to rent a diamond-bladed masonry saw. Cut carefully and be sure to wear protective eyewear. Cut the pipe to 54 inches in length. At one end, cut out a 12-by-12-inch opening.

The chimney may weigh as much as 800 pounds, and it must be set after the concrete footing has cured for a week or so. Consider having the supplier deliver it. You may be able to move it yourself if you have a heavy-duty truck, several helpers, and a come-along.

Have a sheet-metal shop manufacture two heavy steel parts for you: a curved, flat shelf to support the bricks over the opening between the chimney and the fire pit, and a lid with a handle for the top of the chimney.

1 Pour the Footing

See pages 108–111 for instructions on forming and pouring a concrete footing. Excavate for a curved concrete slab that is at least 6 inches deep. You may be able to simply pour into a carefully dug hole in the ground, or you may need to construct curved forms. The pad is in the shape of a figure eight with a small and large loop. The smaller circle should be about 6 inches larger in diameter than the concrete drainpipe. Set in pieces of 12-inch steel reinforcing bar, crisscrossed on 12-inch centers. Pour the

concrete and allow it to cure for a week or so.

2 Place the Drainpipe

Set the drainpipe on top of the slab. Because of its weight, it isn't necessary to mortar it in place. Make sure the opening at the bottom of the drainpipe faces the fire pit.

3 Install the Hanging Bars

About 6 inches from the top, drill four ½-inch holes in the chimney and slide in two pieces of ½-inch reinforcing bar. These will be used for hanging the meat.

4 Cut the Bricks

Cut five or six bricks for the chimney section (with ¾-inch bevels) and five or six for the firebox. Then lay them in a dry run to ensure that the bevels are correct. Cut each brick into thirds with bevel cuts, as shown below. To achieve even mortar lines, you may need to adjust the angle of the cuts.

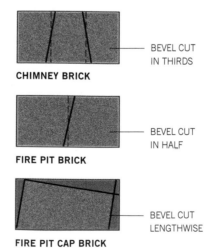

CHIMNEY BRICK — BEVEL CUT IN THIRDS

FIRE PIT BRICK — BEVEL CUT IN HALF

FIRE PIT CAP BRICK — BEVEL CUT LENGTHWISE

MATERIALS LIST

- 3"-thick concrete drainpipe, 54" long × 22" diameter
- Concrete for footing
- ½" steel reinforcing bar, for the footing and for the hanging bars
- Benderboard and stakes
- Common bricks
- Mortar mix
- Firebricks
- Refractory mortar
- Custom metal lid
- Custom metal shelf

5 Lay the Chimney Bricks

See pages 118–121 for instructions on laying bricks. Facing a curved section is tricky because you cannot string a line to check for level. Spread mortar onto the cylinder, no more than 4 square feet at a time, and press the bricks into it. Every few bricks, measure up from the concrete slab and check with a level to make sure you are maintaining level and straight lines. Strike and clean joints as you go.

6 Build the Fire Pit

On the slab for the fire pit, lay the first course of bricks in a mortar bed and then add the remaining two courses. Cut and lay upright firebricks to line the inside of the pit. Cut cap bricks lengthwise using the same angle you used for the bricks below, then lay them on top. Strike and clean the bricks.

stackable barbecue kit

A churrasco barbecue is basically a fireplace with its firebox at a convenient height for cooking (see page 17 for the benefits of churrasco cooking). Building one from scratch requires extensive masonry skills, but if you purchase a kit with stackable components, assembly is fairly easy. Similar kits are available to make a fireplace or a pizza oven. See the resource guide at the back of this book to find suppliers of both these kits and the rotisserie inserts.

THE DESIGN

The components of the kit are made of refractory concrete, which stands up to intense heat and has excellent qualities for cooking (see page 76 for more information on this material). This unit is just the right size for a churrasco-style rotisserie. If you need to vent smoke out a roof or just farther up in the air, you can buy chimney extensions.

Above: *A Spanish-style stucco structure with bright tiles neatly houses a fireplace and rotisserie for churrasco-style cooking.* DESIGNED AND BUILT BY SERGIO DE PAULA, FOGAZZO WOOD FIRED OVENS & BBQS

GETTING READY

The unit will probably weigh a little over a ton when faced with tiles or stucco, so it is a good idea to pour a small reinforced concrete slab to support it (see pages 108–111). Order the kit to be delivered to your home. Once the concrete slab has cured, uncrate the kit and position the stand. Check that the stand is free of wobbles and is level in both directions. If it is not, you may need to cut one or more of the legs, or slip metal shims under one or more legs.

MATERIALS LIST

- Stackable concrete barbecue kit
- Rotisserie kit
- Concrete and reinforcing bar for a small footing
- Metal shims
- Angle brackets
- Masonry screws
- Type S mortar
- Refractory mortar
- Thinset mortar
- Ceramic or stone tile
- Tile grout

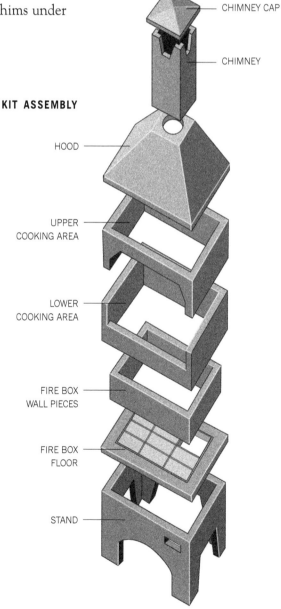

KIT ASSEMBLY

CHIMNEY CAP

CHIMNEY

HOOD

UPPER COOKING AREA

LOWER COOKING AREA

FIRE BOX WALL PIECES

FIRE BOX FLOOR

STAND

1 Set the Firebox Floor

Set each leg of the stand in a dollop of mortar. Anchor each leg with an angle bracket and masonry screws. Mix a small batch of type S concrete and butter the top of the stand as you would a concrete block (see pages 112–113 and 115). Set the firebox floor in the mortar. Scrape away excess mortar and use a masonry jointer to tool the joints as you would on a brick wall (see page 121).

2 Stack the Pieces with Mortar

Spread mortar on the lip of the stand and set the lower cooking area piece in the mortar. Check for level in both directions. If it is not level, tap one side with a rubber mallet or lift the piece up and add mortar in one or more places. Scrape away excess mortar and tool the joints. Continue stacking the pieces, checking each for level and plumb and tooling the joints as you go.

3 Set the Firebox Inner Wall

Spread refractory mortar around the perimeter of the firebox floor and insert each of the four inner wall pieces, which fit around the floor. Apply refractory mortar to fill the gaps between the wall pieces and between the walls and the floor.

4 Tile the Upper Cooking Area

This is optional, but it adds a great deal to the look of the barbecue. See pages 130–131 for general instructions on installing tiles. You may choose to install bullnose tiles for the edges or just use field tiles for a more rustic look. Install tiles in the upper cooking area and around the hearth. Set them in latex or polymer-fortified thinset mortar and fill the joints with latex-fortified grout.

5 Prepare for Stucco

To ensure that the stucco will not crack, cut pieces of metal stucco lath to fit, then attach them to the sides of the barbecue by drilling holes and driving short masonry screws with galvanized washers. Cut and install the lath carefully so that it is no more than $\frac{3}{8}$ inch from the surface at any point.

6 Apply Stucco

Cover the tiles with masking tape and newspaper to protect them while you are stuccoing. See pages 126–127 for general instructions on applying stucco. Apply a base coat that covers the metal lath. Allow the stucco to cure slowly over two or three days. Then apply a second coat and follow that with a third. It is best to mix the finish coat with integral color rather than paint the stucco, because paint may peel in areas that get very hot.

95

full-service kitchen

The kitchen has it all: a pizza oven, a sink with running water, a large grill, a side burner, warming trays, and a refrigerator—plus a spacious overhead structure. An ambitious installation like this is generally best left to pros. The following six pages break the project into steps to show how construction typically proceeds on a big job.

THE DESIGN

The main section of the L-shaped counter is about 10 feet long—enough to accommodate the appliances with a modest amount of counter space. The leg of the L, which is 4 feet long, provides additional countertop space. Because the appliances and doors must fit into a tight space, the builder chose to make the front wall out of cast concrete rather than concrete block. A concrete wall can be formed in just about any shape. The other counter walls are built of 6-inch concrete block. The backsplash is framed with wood. A 2-inch-thick steel-

This L-shaped counter includes a Spanish-style pizza oven at one end. The counter houses a wealth of cooking amenities to make outdoor meals an easy-to-prepare everyday pleasure. DESIGN: SERGIO DE PAULA, FOGAZZO WOOD FIRED OVENS & BBQS

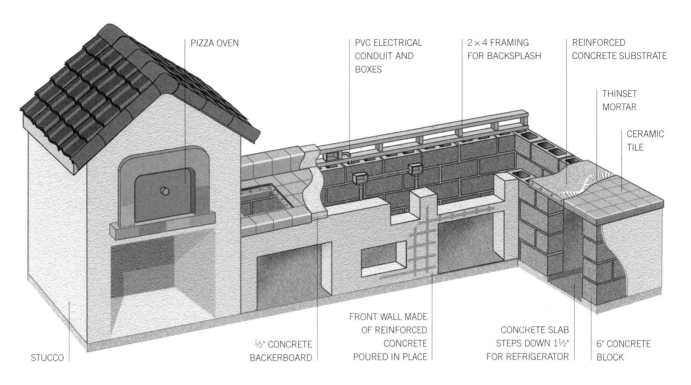

PIZZA OVEN

PVC ELECTRICAL CONDUIT AND BOXES

2 × 4 FRAMING FOR BACKSPLASH

REINFORCED CONCRETE SUBSTRATE

THINSET MORTAR

CERAMIC TILE

STUCCO

½" CONCRETE BACKERBOARD

FRONT WALL MADE OF REINFORCED CONCRETE POURED IN PLACE

CONCRETE SLAB STEPS DOWN 1½" FOR REFRIGERATOR

6" CONCRETE BLOCK

TO SUPPORT THE GRILL, SEE PAGES 106–107

reinforced concrete substrate is poured and allowed to cure, then covered with salmon-colored ceramic tile set in thinset mortar.

Quite a few utility lines run into a counter like this. A gas line feeds both the grill and the side burner. A water line runs to the area beneath the sink, where it hooks up to an on-demand water heater to supply both hot and cold water. The drain line leads to the house's main sewer line. Electricity powers a receptacle on the backsplash, as well as receptacles inside the counter for the warming drawer, the grill's rotisserie, and the refrigerator.

To the left of the counter is a pizza oven made of refractory concrete. The oven is housed in a structure made of concrete block and rests on a raised concrete slab. For instructions on building an oven like this, see pages 76–79. The oven is topped with a tile roof. Both the oven and the counter are covered with white stucco.

GETTING READY

If you will hire a professional installer, see page 36 for tips on choosing a contractor and drawing up a contract. For a project like this you will need to get the

plans approved by your local building department and schedule several inspections.

In most cases, you should plan the overhead structure along with the counter and oven, and decide at which stage you will install the posts. In this case, the posts were installed after the walls were built, but sometimes it's easier to set the posts when you make the footing.

Have all the appliances and doors on hand, and draw your plans carefully to be sure everything will fit. As you build, periodically test to make sure everything will fit.

1 Excavate and Trench

To get all those utility lines to the counter area, you will need to dig trenches (see pages 108–109). Consult local codes to learn how deep the trenches need to be, as well as which types of cable, pipe, and conduit are required. Call your utility companies before you start to dig, to avoid accidentally breaking a gas, water, or electrical line. The contractor will run the drain line either to the house drain, the city storm drain, or a dry well. Expect this process to create plenty of rubble and arrange for its removal. If you need to cut a channel in a concrete slab, plan to patch the hole when you pour the concrete for the footing.

2 Build Forms

Construct a form out of 2 by 4s. Anchor the boards to a concrete surface using metal brackets and masonry nails or screws. Anchor the boards to the ground using metal form stakes. In this installation, the concrete footing rises 3½ inches above the ground, which can make it easier to frame for doors. However, note that the footing must be lower where the refrigerator will go.

MATERIALS LIST

FOR THE COUNTER:
- Grill
- Side burner
- Outdoor cabinet doors
- Refrigerator
- Warming drawer unit
- Gas pipe, shutoff valve, and connections
- Electrical supplies: cable or conduit with wire, boxes, GFCI receptacles
- Plumbing supplies: drain lines, supply line, stop valves
- On-demand water heater
- Concrete for the footing
- 6" × 8" × 16" Concrete block
- ½" reinforcing bar with chairs to hold the pieces up
- Mortar mix
- Metal studs and channels
- Masonry screws
- Stucco mix
- ½" concrete backerboard
- 2 × 6s and ¾" plywood to build the form for the front wall
- Ceramic tiles
- Latex-reinforced thinset mortar
- Silicone caulk
- Acrylic masonry sealer

FOR THE PIZZA OVEN:
- Materials as listed on page 76

FOR THE OVERHEAD:
- 4 × 4s and 2 × 6s for posts
- Concrete for the postholes
- 2 × 8s for the beams
- 2 × 8s for the rafters
- 2 × 2s for the top pieces
- 7" carriage bolts with nuts and washers
- 3" deck screws
- Redwood deck stain

3 Run the Lines and Add Rebar

Carefully plan the routes for the plumbing, gas, and electrical lines so that they exit the concrete slab at convenient locations. In most cases, the lines should emerge an inch or so inside the rear block wall. Make sure the drain line is sloped at a rate of at least $1/4$ inch per foot. Think through how you will continue the lines and hook them to appliances or receptacles after the walls are built.

Install a grid of rebar, tying the pieces together with wire and holding them off the ground with concrete pieces (as shown) or metal "chairs." If you will reinforce the blocks with concrete and rebar, mark the form boards for the locations of the vertical rebar running through the centers of every two or three cells. Use a rebar bender to bend the bar up.

4 Pour the Concrete

Once you are sure of the locations of the utility lines and the rebar, order concrete for delivery. You can pour it into the forms using wheelbarrows, but it is usually worth the extra cost to arrange for the concrete to be supplied in a tube, as shown. Pouring may cause the vertical rebar pieces to move, so check them for alignment and adjust as needed.

5 Finish the Concrete

Use a piece of level 2 by 4 to screed the concrete, then use a magnesium float to further smooth it (see pages 110–111).

If bleed water appears on the surface, wait for it to nearly evaporate before smoothing. Again, check the rebar pieces for correct alignment. Cover the concrete with plastic or periodically spray it with a fine mist so it slowly cures over several days. (The slower the cure, the stronger the concrete.)

6 Lay the First Course

See pages 114–117 for instructions on building a block counter. In this installation, an extra-strong method is used. The first course is made of blocks with special cutouts, and $1/2$-inch rebar is run through the cutouts. In most cases, ladder-style reinforcing is sufficient.

7 Build Up the Walls

Continue building the walls, striking the joints as you go. Use a mason's block and line, as well as a level, to keep the walls straight and level. Fill the cells with a wet concrete mixture. Here, long rebar protrudes up through the pizza oven walls. In this installation, the front wall for the main counter section will be poured later (see step 11).

8 Build the Pizza Oven

Follow the instructions on pages 76–79 for building the pizza oven. After the walls are built to a height of 4 feet, a reinforced concrete slab is poured. Then the oven kit is assembled, walls are built upward, the chimney is installed, and the roof is built.

9 Install Posts and Beams

See pages 150–153 for general instructions on building an overhead. Use rot-resistant lumber. Lay out for six posts that form a rectangle and then dig postholes at least 3 feet deep. Set in the 4-by-4 posts, check them for alignment, temporarily brace them so they are plumb, and pour concrete into the postholes. (You will cut the posts to height later.) Once the concrete has cured for two days or so, cut and attach 2 by 6s on opposite sides of each post so that their tops are all at the same height. Cut 2-by-8 beams to length, with decorative cuts at each end. Set the beams on top of the 2 by 6s and attach them with two carriage bolts at each post.

10 Add the Rafters and Top Pieces

Cut 2-by-8 rafters to fit on top of the beams so that they overhang the same amount as the beams. Install them with carriage bolts. Top the structure with evenly spaced 2 by 2s. Attach the top pieces to the rafters using deck screws.

11 Install Electrical Boxes and Build the Front Wall

Run conduit, install electrical boxes, and pull wires for the receptacles (see pages 142–143). Build a form for the concrete using 2 by 6s sandwiched between pieces of ¾-inch plywood. Run rebar through the form, taking special care to reinforce the narrow horizontal sections. Anchor the form to the rear wall and check that it is straight. Spray or brush oil on the wood so it will not stick to the concrete. Pour concrete into the form and use a concrete vibrator to make sure the concrete settles into every nook and cranny. Remove the forms the next day and keep the concrete damp so it cures over several days.

12 Frame the Backsplash and Apply Stucco

To support the counter's back-splash, build a short wall using 2 by 4s. Anchor the bottom plate to the block wall by setting bolts in concrete-filled cells. On the rear of the counter, install a con-tinuous piece of concrete backer-board. Fasten it by driving screws into the wood framing, and spread thinset mortar to attach it to the blocks. Mount the receptacle box in the framing. Apply stucco in two or three coats (see pages 126–127).

13 Pour a Reinforced Concrete Countertop Substrate

Construct a temporary form using backerboard or plywood and 2 by 4s. Frame around the opening for the sink and the small grill, and use metal studs or another method to permanently frame the support for the large grill (see pages 106–107). Add a grid of reinforcing bar, and pour the concrete (see pages 136–139).

14 Tile

See pages 132–135 for instruc-tions on installing countertop tile. Lay the tiles in a dry run and make all the cuts. Working one section at a time, spread thinset mortar and set the tiles, using plastic spacers to maintain straight joint lines. You may need to use tape to hold the edging pieces until the mortar sets.

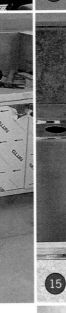

15 Set the Sink

See pages 144–147 for instructions on installing a sink. Notice the tile detail on the backsplash, which uses four triangular pieces of field tile and one decorative tile tilted 45 degrees.

16 Finish Up

Apply grout and wipe it clean. Install the grill and the side burner (see pages 148–149), and then plug in the refrig-erator. Install doors and drawers.

how to build them

MOST OF THE PROJECTS IN CHAPTER 2 involve quite a variety of building techniques: pouring and finishing concrete, building with block, running utility lines, hooking up wiring and plumbing, and various ways to finish the counters and countertops. While some of this construction may look intimidating, this chapter will show you how to divide the work into discrete, manageable tasks. If you take them one at a time, you may be surprised to find that most are within your reach. Or you may decide to hire professional builders for some or all of the work. Don't forget to contact your local building department to make sure you are in compliance with structural, electrical, and plumbing codes. Regulations may demand that certain tasks, such as making basic wiring and gas connections, be done only by a licensed professional.

tools

A barbecue counter may be built with any combination of block, stone, brick, backerboard, wood studs, steel studs, granite, and tile. Here you will find some of the tools most commonly used for building a counter.

A collection of tools like these is inexpensive compared with the cost of hiring a pro, so don't hesitate to spend a little more for professional-quality tools. A high-quality tool will make the job easier and provide superior results.

CARPENTRY A basic set of carpentry tools comes in handy for most any project. Use a carpenter's square to check corners. A 25-foot tape measure will handle most jobs. Use a carpenter's level to check walls for level and plumb. A chalk line quickly marks straight lines. Drive screws and bore pilot holes with a drill. Use a caulk gun to seal joints at the end of a job.

MASONRY To quickly align blocks or bricks as you lay them, hook a mason's corner block to a block or brick at each end and stretch a mason's line between them. Use a mason's (or brick) trowel to spread mortar. A margin trowel is the ideal tool to mix a small amount of mortar in a bucket and to scoop it out as well. A magnesium or Teflon float is the best tool for a beginner to use when smoothing wet concrete. Use a concrete edger to round off the corners of a concrete slab.

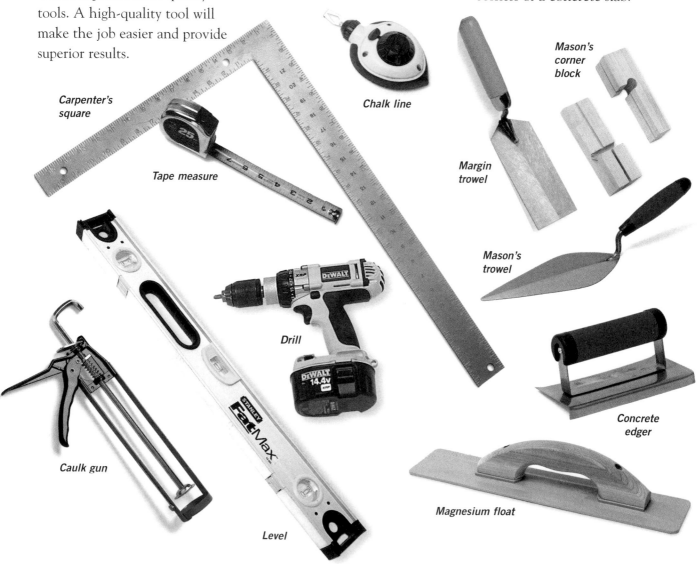

Carpenter's square

Chalk line

Mason's corner block

Margin trowel

Tape measure

Mason's trowel

Drill

Concrete edger

Caulk gun

Magnesium float

Level

TILING You can make straight cuts in many types of ceramic tile using a snap cutter. Cut other types with a wet-cutting masonry saw (see page 130). To spread thinset mortar, use a notched trowel of the size recommended for your tiles. With a laminated grout float you can easily press grout into joints and then squeegee most of it away. A rubber mallet is often the best tool for embedding tiles in mortar.

WIRING Most wiring requires few special tools. A reliable tester is a must, to make sure power is off before you start work. A good pair of wire strippers will enable you to quickly strip insulation off wire ends without damaging the wire. Use lineman's pliers to cut wire and to twist wires together when you make splices.

PLUMBING Buy all the tools you need to cut and join the types of pipe you have chosen. Use a tubing cutter to cut copper pipe and a propane torch to solder copper fittings. A large pair of slip-joint pliers will grip and tighten most any type of pipe, including drain traps. Use PVC cutters to cut plastic pipe and rubber tubing up to 1 inch in diameter. Use a PVC saw to cut larger plastic pipes.

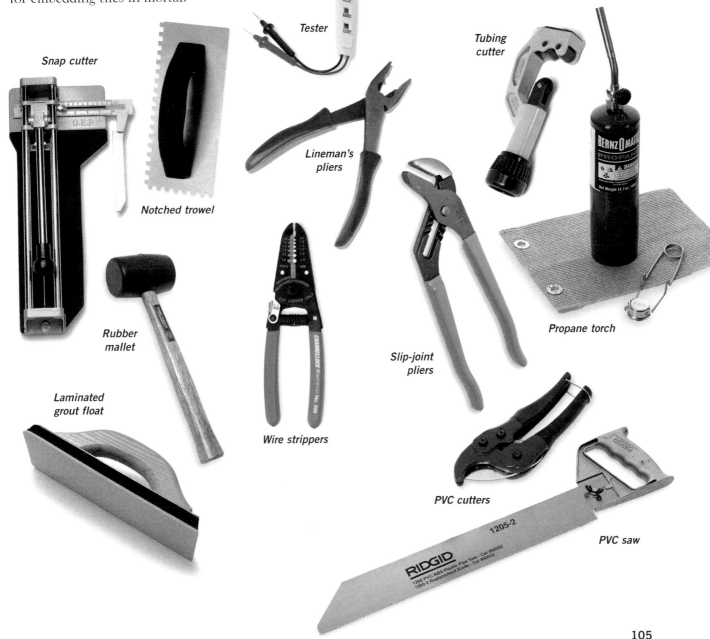

Snap cutter

Notched trowel

Tester

Lineman's pliers

Tubing cutter

Propane torch

Rubber mallet

Laminated grout float

Wire strippers

Slip-joint pliers

PVC cutters

PVC saw

planning the grill opening

Some manufacturers specify that a grill must reside in an enclosure consisting of three walls and a bottom support. The enclosure will typically have an opening in the rear for running the fuel line.

THE RIGHT HEIGHT

The support must be at the correct height for the grill to be comfortable to use and for the flange to rest on the countertop. With many grills, the flange can be adjusted up or down or even installed separately, so there is some leeway.

To plan the height of the support, consider the total thickness of the countertop. The illustration below shows the types of measurements you will need to make. This countertop has two layers of $\frac{1}{2}$-inch backerboard topped with ceramic tile. The tile is $\frac{3}{8}$ inch thick, and there are

A heavy barbecue grill must rest on a strong support that is at the correct height. This sometimes presents design challenges, which these two pages address. Carefully read the installation specs for your grill to be sure it will fit and will be adequately supported.

This grill opening is supported underneath and sealed all around, as required by the manufacturer. Before the grill is installed, a hole will be drilled or cut to make room for the gas line.

SUPPORTS AND SURROUNDS

Smaller and lighter grills can simply rest, via flanges on three sides, on the countertop with no support from underneath. If your grill is this type, build a strong countertop and ignore the remainder of these two pages. If your grill needs support from below, then read on.

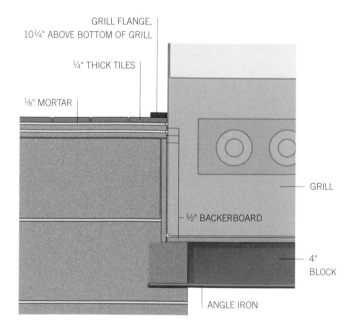

GRILL FLANGE, 10¼" ABOVE BOTTOM OF GRILL

¼" THICK TILES

⅛" MORTAR

GRILL

½" BACKERBOARD

4" BLOCK

ANGLE IRON

two layers of ⅛-inch-thick mortar—for a total thickness of 1⅝ inches. This grill flange is 10¼ inches above the bottom of the grill. That means the grill support should be 8⅝ inches below the top of the concrete block. If the lintel is made of 4-inch block topped with ½-inch backerboard, then the angle iron under the lintel should be 13⅛ inches below the top of the concrete block.

SUPPORT OPTIONS

Grill manufacturers typically tell you to provide a solid support but don't always say how. Here are three possible solutions, illustrated at right.

STEEL FRAMING AND BACKERBOARD

See pages 122–123 for instructions on cutting and joining steel framing. To build a platform for the grill, attach channels to the front and rear wall at the same height as the lintel using masonry screws. Then cut and attach studs running between the channels. Once you screw backerboard on top of the framing, the platform will be very strong. You can build walls using the same materials.

POURED CONCRETE AND BLOCK

This is not as complicated as it may appear. Construct short block walls inside the counter to support the concrete slab. Lay backerboard on top of the walls, temporarily support it from underneath with plywood and

This grill has a flange that is adjustable up and down, but only by an inch or so. Carefully sealed with caulk, it will keep the area below fairly dry during rainfalls.

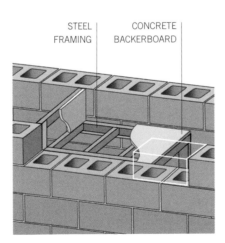

STEEL FRAMING AND BACKERBOARD

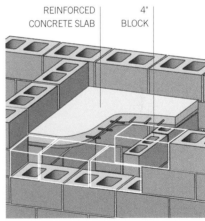

POURED CONCRETE AND BLOCK

vertical 2 by 4s, add steel reinforcement, and pour a concrete slab (see pages 136–139).

STEEL PLATE Build walls similar to those for the concrete slab. Purchase a sheet of ¼-inch steel from a fabricator, lay it on top, and add a layer of ½-inch concrete backerboard.

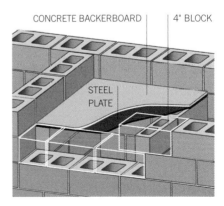

STEEL PLATE

running utility lines

A full-service outdoor kitchen may require a gas line, conduit for electrical wiring, water supply pipe, and a water drain line. Most people hire pros to dig the trenches, run the lines, and make the hookups to the house, even if they finish the final hookups inside the counter themselves. Make sure your lines are run and attached in accordance with local building codes, which vary widely by area.

DIGGING TRENCHES AND PROTECTING PIPES

In many regions, codes allow pipes to be run in trenches 12 inches deep, but your building department may require deeper trenches. Before digging, check with your utility companies to make sure you will not accidentally break any gas, electrical, or plumbing lines. Digging can be

This trench holds black ABS drainpipe, copper water supply pipe, black gas pipe, and PVC conduit for the electrical line.

difficult work; a power trencher will ease the task. Cut through a concrete slab using a rented gas-powered masonry cutoff saw. Once the lines are run and the trench is filled, patch the slab with new concrete.

To protect pipes, codes may require that you wrap some in foam insulation. In some areas, laying pressure-treated 2-by lumber over the pipes will allow you to dig shallower trenches. Make sure the drain line will be sloped.

GAS LINE

A natural gas line must be connected to the house's gas pipe somewhere after the meter, and there should be a separate shutoff valve for the outdoor line. Consult the gas company to see if this should be done inside or outside. It may be best to have the gas company install a fitting and a shutoff valve, to which you will connect the pipe.

Yellow gas pipe, made of corrugated stainless steel wrapped with yellow vinyl, is the top choice in many areas. It is fairly flexible, and warming it in the sun before use will make it more so, but it will not be able to make tight turns. If possible, snake it through trenches and up through the counter's slab. Install the compression-type fittings only above ground.

Black gas pipe, made of steel, is also common (see left). Though

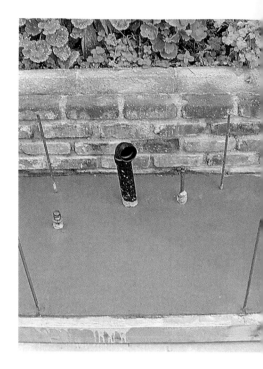

Plan so that the drain, gas pipe, water line, and electrical conduit poke up at locations convenient for installing the appliances and plumbing.

steel rusts, this is not a problem for underground lines that are not exposed to oxygen. This is a rigid pipe, so fittings must be installed underground. Connect the pipes and fittings using a pair of pipe wrenches. Be sure to wrap the male ends of the pipes with yellow Teflon tape, made for gas pipe, before connecting the fittings.

WIRING

Consult Sunset's *Complete Home Wiring* to make sure the electrical line you run will not overload the circuit it is connected to. The simplest solution is to connect the wiring to an outdoor receptacle or to an easily reached indoor receptacle. If your kitchen will use a lot of electricity, or if there is no easily accessible circuit, run the wiring into the service panel and connect it to a new circuit breaker. Hire a pro for this unless you are confident in your abilities.

PVC conduit is the most common choice for protecting electrical lines. For the safest installation, run conduit all the way from the house, through trenches, and up through the counter floor. Then run either individual wires or underground cable through the conduit. Many local codes allow you to run underground cable (labeled "UF") through the trenches and to use conduit only for the portions that run up through the counter's slab at one end and to the house connection at the other end.

WATER SUPPLY PIPES

In many cases, one cold-water supply pipe is run through to the counter. There it branches out and connects to an on-demand water heater to supply both cold and hot water to the faucet. However, if the counter is near the house, you may run both a cold and a hot water pipe from the house to the counter.

It is often most convenient to hook up the supply line near an outdoor hose bib or near the water meter, but you can tap into most any supply pipe. A shutoff valve should control each pipe that leads to the counter.

In areas with freezing winters, follow local codes to ensure that supply pipes will not freeze and burst. If you live in such an area, you may need to purge the lines before winter. Either run the lines so they are sloped and install special bleed valves at the low points, or use an air compressor to blow water out of the lines.

Solid copper is a common supply pipe. See page 145 for how to cut and join copper pipe and fittings. CPVC plastic pipe is another common material. It joins with primer and glue.

For a simple supply line, run a dedicated garden hose into the counter and connect it to the faucet. Add an on-demand water heater if you want hot water.

DRAIN LINE

A kitchen sink's drain typically carries only soapy or dirty water, so code requirements may not be as strict as those for other drain lines. Depending on your site and local codes, the drainpipe may run into the house's main drain, the municipal sewer system, or a city storm drain.

The line must slope consistently downhill at a rate of $1/4$ inch or more per foot. Codes may require that it be vented, meaning that it be tied to a vertical pipe that supplies air. A vent pipe may tie to pipes that lead up and out the house's roof. Another venting arrangement uses a short pipe that comes out of the ground and is topped with a special fitting that protects the pipe but allows air in.

Before you plunge into complicated planning, see if you can simply run the drain line into a dry well (see below). This slowly disperses drain water into the yard, which is fine as long as you do not run the faucet for long periods or use a lot of dishwashing soap.

To make a dry well, drill a grid of 1-inch holes in a 10-gallon plastic bucket. Near the top, drill a larger hole for the drainpipe. Dig a hole about 6 inches deeper than the bucket and set the bucket in the hole. Fill it with rocks and run the drain line through a trench into the bucket. Cover the bucket with landscaping fabric, soil, and sod.

A dry well is the simplest way to deal with drain water.

pouring a concrete slab

A heavy outdoor counter must rest on a solid foundation. In most cases, this means a reinforced concrete slab that is thick enough to satisfy local codes. In the most common arrangement, the perimeter of the slab, which supports the counter walls and is called the footing, is thicker than the interior, which acts as the counter's floor. If you want a very smooth finish, hire a concrete finisher. A do-it-yourselfer can produce a surface that is smooth enough for the inside of a counter (see step 4). For more detailed instructions on mixing, pouring, and finishing a concrete slab, see Sunset's *Complete Patio Book*.

1 Excavate and Build the Form

Mark out the area for the slab, then dig up the sod and any other organic material such as roots. Build a form using 2 by 4s, set it onto the excavated area, and check it for square and level. In most cases, the slab should be slightly above grade or above an adjoining patio surface. Anchor the form boards with stakes every few feet. Drive the stakes slightly below the top of the form boards. The boards should feel solid when you kick them outward.

Stretch mason's lines across the tops of the form boards and use them as guides as you continue digging to the final depth of the slab. When you reach the bottom of the excavation, stop digging and instead scrape down so you do not loosen the soil. Tamp the soil with a hand tamper or a length of 4 by 4. Spread 2 or 3 inches of compactible gravel in the bottom of the excavation and tamp it as well.

Run any pipes and conduit into the formed area, as shown on pages 108–109. A board-and-clamp arrangement, shown on the opposite page in step 4, helps keep the pipes in place.

2 Pour the Concrete

To calculate the amount of concrete you will need, tell a supplier the dimensions of the excavation. If you need more than ¾ cubic

yard, it is usually best to order the concrete delivered in a ready-mix truck. For smaller amounts, you can mix it yourself in a wheelbarrow using bags of dry-mix concrete. Some local codes require wire mesh or reinforcing bar, but you may be able to avoid this if you order concrete with fiberglass reinforcement. A ready-mix truck's chute might be able to reach into the formed area. If not, or if you are mixing your own, put down board paths for wheelbarrows. Have a helper or two wheel and dump the concrete into the formed area while you use a shovel to scrape and spread it.

3 Screed

Once the concrete has filled the form, set a straight 2 by 4 across the form boards and screed the concrete by dragging the board across the surface. Move the board in a sawing motion as you pull it. Where the concrete is low, sprinkle on small amounts with a shovel, then screed again.

4 Smooth with a Float

Wait for any pools of water, called bleed water or cream, to evaporate before you rework the surface. Use a magnesium or Teflon float to smooth the surface. Hold the tool so that the leading edge is slightly raised, pressing down gently as you work. Use long, sweeping motions as much as possible.

5 Edge and Cure

Slip a mason's trowel between the form boards and the concrete and slice along the perimeter of the slab to eliminate air pockets that can weaken the concrete. To further eliminate air pockets, tap the form boards with a hammer all along their length. Run a concrete edging tool along the perimeter of the slab to round off the top edge. Once bleed water evaporates, smooth the surface again with the float.

The more slowly concrete cures, the stronger it will be. After finishing, keep the concrete moist for at least several days. Cover the slab with plastic or spray it with a fine mist twice a day. After a day, carefully pry away the forms.

working with mortar and block

A professional mason can "throw" a neat line of mortar on blocks or bricks with amazing speed and consistency. Unless you have experience building masonry walls, you will not be able to do that. But with a bit of practice you can spread mortar in even lines that are the right thickness. You may never be as fast as a pro, but the result will be a wall that is straight and sound.

The counter shown on pages 114–117 uses 6-inch-thick block, which is the most commonly used material. However, you may choose to use 8- or 4-inch block instead. Depending on your locale, you may find stretchers (the blocks used in the middle of walls) with webbed ends or with solid ends. You'll also need full-size end blocks, which have one finished end, and half blocks, which are finished on all four sides. Also buy angle irons and solid 2- or 4-inch-thick blocks for above and below the openings. The thinner blocks may be available only in 8-inch widths, so you'll have to cut them narrower if you are building with 6-inch block. You may use bent pieces of rebar to tie adjoining walls together (see page 115, step 5), or reinforce the walls using ladder-style horizontal wire or vertical rebar (see pages 116, step 6, and 117, step 12).

MIXING MORTAR

You can mix a small amount of mortar in a bucket using a margin trowel. For larger amounts, use a wheelbarrow and a mason's hoe. Pour about 1/3 bag of mortar mix into the container. Add water a little at a time and mix with the hoe. Try not to mix more mortar than you will be able to use before it starts to harden.

Some common types of concrete block (clockwise from top): 8" webbed stretcher; 6" solid-end stretcher; solid 2" and 4" blocks; half block; 4" block; and 6" corner block. You'll also need mortar mix, angle iron, ladder-type reinforcement, and pieces of rebar.

It's critical to achieve just the right mortar consistency. The mortar must be wet enough to stick but dry enough to hold its shape and not run down the side of the wall. Here are two tests:

1. Cut ridges in the mortar with a mason's trowel. The ridges should hold their shape, but the mortar should not appear crumbly.

2. Scoop some mortar with a mason's trowel or margin trowel and hold it upside down. The mortar should stick to the trowel for a second or two, then slide off.

If the mortar is too dry or too wet, add water or dry mix. If the mortar starts to harden or develop crumbs while you work, throw it out and make a new batch.

CUTTING BLOCK

Cutting concrete block is not as difficult as you may think, but it will create plenty of dust. Equip a high-quality circular saw with an inexpensive abrasive masonry blade, which will likely wear down after cutting four or five blocks, or a longer-lasting diamond blade. Protect yourself with a respirator, protective eyewear, ear plugs, and gloves. Set the blade to the right thickness and cut the block. Work slowly. If the saw heats up, take a break to allow it to cool.

SURFACE-BONDED BLOCK

Here's a method that saves time, requires no special skills, and creates a wall nearly as strong as one with mortared joints. Set the bottom row of blocks in a bed of mortar (see pages 114–115, steps 1 and 2). Then simply stack the remaining blocks without using mortar. Once all the blocks are stacked, mix a batch of surface-bonding mortar, place a shovelful on a hawk or a piece of plywood, and use a flat trowel to smear it onto both sides of the wall. Aim for a fairly smooth surface. Allow the mortar to dry, then apply a second coat and create the stucco texture of your choice (see pages 126–127).

building a block counter

Concrete block is not as easy to cut and assemble as wood or steel framing, but you may find it less difficult than you expected. Six-inch blocks are only moderately heavy, so the work is not physically demanding. The important thing is to plan carefully. The block wall should rest on a firm concrete slab that is level and thick enough to satisfy local building codes (see pages 110–111).

BUILDING BASICS

Buy bags of dry mortar mix, which contain the right combination of portland cement, sand, and sometimes lime. Type N mortar is strong enough for most projects. For extra strength, or if part of the installation will get soaked in water, buy type S. Depending on the size of the job, mix the mortar in a wheelbarrow, a plastic trough, or a bucket. Either scoop the mortar with your trowel directly out of the container you mixed it in, or load a shovelful onto a hawk or a piece of plywood about 16 inches square to make it easier to carry around.

Make a detailed drawing that shows each block. Aim to minimize cuts. For instance, if the wall is 32 inches wide, you can use all full- and half-sized blocks.

Standard 6-inch block cannot interlock at the corners (as 8-inch block can). Either tie the walls together with bent pieces of rebar and/or ladder-type horizontal wire (steps 5 and 6) or use special 6-inch corner blocks.

A simple block wall with mortared joints will provide sufficient support for most purposes. For extra strength, and perhaps to satisfy local codes, you can use ladder-type horizontal reinforcing. You can also run vertical rebar through some of the cells and fill the cells with concrete. For the ultimate in strength, run vertical rebar up through the concrete slab every few cells. Also run horizontal rebar and then fill all the cells with concrete (see pages 99–100). Because the walls are tied together, you will probably need to build all the walls up at once instead of finishing one wall and then moving on to the next.

Professional masons apply mortar using a triangular brick trowel or mason's trowel. With this tool, they can literally throw the mortar onto the blocks. If you are a novice, you may find it easier to smear the mortar using a margin trowel. A rubber mallet comes in handy for leveling blocks that are set in mortar.

1 Lay Out and Spread a Bed of Mortar

Snap chalk lines that are a consistent distance—1 or 2 inches—from each side of the blocks. Use a pencil to mark the openings exactly, then double-check that the openings are the correct width. Use a framing square to check the corners. Dampen the slab. Mix a batch of mortar and spread a layer about $\frac{1}{2}$ inch thick in between the layout lines.

2 Bed and Level the First Block

Set an end block or a half block in the mortar bed, centered between the chalk lines and exactly aligned with the end line. (You may need to scrape away mortar to see the line.) Press it into place so that the mortar is about ⅜ inch thick. Check the block for level in both directions and check the face of the end for plumb. Scrape away excess mortar and use it for the next block.

3 Butter a Block End

Scrape mortar onto the end (or the end webs, if you are using webbed stringers) of the next block to form peaks as shown. On a long wall, you should set an end block at the other end first, then set up a string line and fill in between the two blocks (see step 7). For a short wall like this, simply set the blocks in order.

4 Check for Straightness and Level

Set the next block in place and push it against the first block so that the joint between them is about ⅜ inch. Check the block for level. Scrape mortar onto the flanges of the laid blocks and set the next course of blocks on top. Start the next row with a corner block or a half block, so the blocks will be stacked one on top of two. Check this row for level and see that the blocks form a straight line. Scrape mortar from the joints as you work.

5 Tie a Corner Together

If you don't use corner blocks, you can use this method. Where two walls adjoin, use a circular saw with a masonry blade to cut channels in the tops of the blocks. Bend a piece of rebar to fit. Fill the cells with mortar and set the rebar in the mortar. Do this every other course.

6 Reinforce with Ladder Wire

To strengthen a wall, and perhaps a corner as well, add ladder wire every other course and under the top course. Spread a layer of mortar onto all the webs and set the wire in the mortar.

7 Use a Line Guide for a Long Wall

On a long wall, set the blocks at each end, then attach mason's line to a corner block at each end and pull it taut. Install the intervening blocks so they nearly touch the line. The line can serve as a guide for level as well as straightness along the wall's side.

8 Finish a Long Wall with a Closure Block

The last block on a long wall, called the closure block, is a bit tricky to install. If you need to cut a block, cut the next-to-last block and then install a full-sized closure block. Spread a thick layer of mortar onto both ends of the closure block. Align it precisely with the center of the opening and carefully slide it straight down into place. If mortar peels off one of the ends, pick the closure block up, reapply mortar, and try again.

9 Install an Angle Iron

At a lintel (the top of an opening), install an angle iron for support. If possible, plan the installation so you can set the angle iron on top of a block at each side of the opening. If that is not possible, use a circular saw equipped with a masonry blade to cut a channel that you can slide the lintel into. Mark and cut carefully so the angle iron will be level. The masonry saw blade makes a cut that is just thick enough for the angle iron.

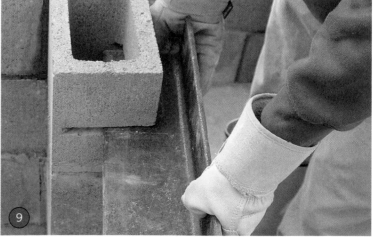

10 Finish a Lintel

Fill the cells on each side of the opening to cement the angle iron in place. Spread mortar and install blocks on the angle iron.

11 Install an Electrical Box

Electrical conduit should run inside the counter, rather than through the block cells, wherever possible. To install an electrical box on the outside of the counter, cut an opening for the box using a circular saw and set the box in so it protrudes the thickness of whatever finish material you will use. Drill a hole for the conduit using a masonry bit. Draw a circle for the conduit's hole, drill six or seven holes along its circumference, then chip out the hole using a small masonry bit. Run conduit to the box using an elbow to make the turn. Tap in shims to wedge the box in place. Stuff newspapers into the cell about 6 inches below the electrical box, then fill the area around the box with concrete to hold the box firmly in place.

12 Strengthen a Wall by Filling It

A narrow wall section like this can be strengthened with concrete and rebar in one or more block cells. Mix a batch of concrete that is wet enough to pour easily. Pour in a foot or so of concrete. Cut a piece of rebar to the height of the wall minus an inch or so and insert it into the center of the cell. Fill the cell the rest of the way with concrete. For extra strength, you can use this method on some or even all of the cells.

If your grill needs to be supported from beneath, see pages 106–107 for grill support options. If you will use two layers of concrete backerboard as a substrate for a tiled countertop (see page 132), support the backerboard with steel studs that span from the front to the rear wall every 16 inches.

building with brick

Brick may be applied in a single width, called a wythe, to the side of a block counter. You can also build a counter entirely of brick laid in two wythes. On a double-wythe wall, you may choose to stack the bricks in a simple running bond—with all the bricks laid lengthwise, one on top of two. For greater strength, lay some of the bricks sideways to tie the wythes together. These sideways bricks, called headers, should be set in regular patterns. For example, the wall on pages 120–121 uses a common bond pattern, in which every fifth course, or layer, is a header course.

A bricklayer can build a straight, strong wall quickly. Unless you have experience, you will probably build much more slowly. But if you work carefully, your wall can be just as strong and straight. A brick wall must rest on a solid concrete footing (see pages 110–111).

THROWING MORTAR AND LAYING BRICKS

1 Throw a Line of Mortar

For instructions on mixing mortar, see pages 112–113. Scoop up mortar with a brick trowel. With the face of the trowel pointing up, snap the trowel downward quickly. The mortar will lift very slightly and make a smacking sound as it settles back onto the trowel. This loosens the mortar's grip on the trowel.

Next comes the tricky part. To throw a line of mortar, fully extend your arm directly in front of you. Rotate the trowel until the mortar starts to slide off, then pull the trowel back toward you. The goal is to deposit mortar in an even line about 1 inch thick, three-quarters of a brick wide, and two or three bricks long. The process should be fairly quick and smooth, and the mortar should hit the bricks with a slight slap.

2 Furrow the Mortar

Turn the trowel on its side and drag its point through the mortar to produce a channel about half the thickness of the mortar line. Take care that the mortar does not slide off the side of the bricks. If that happens, slice the mortar off in the same manner shown in step 5.

3 Butter a Brick End

Every brick except the first in a course needs to have at least one end buttered. To butter, hold a brick in one hand and load the trowel with a small amount of mortar. Scrape the trowel at a 45-degree angle to the brick end and then lightly pull the trowel back. Shape the mortar this way in all four directions.

4 Lay a Brick

Place the brick on the mortar bed, about 2 inches from the brick it will abut, and slide it into place. Ideally, a little mortar will squeeze out of all the joints. Any small gaps at the joints can be filled when you strike the joint (see page 121, step 7). If there are gaps greater than an inch, remove the brick, scrape away the mortar, and start again.

5 Clean Off the Excess

Use the trowel like a knife to slice off the squeezed-out mortar. If you slice quickly and in one motion, little mortar will smear onto the face of the bricks. Every 10 minutes or so (depending on heat and humidity), strike, and perhaps clean, the joints (see page 121, steps 7 and 8).

BUILDING A DOUBLE-WYTHE WALL

1 Set the Bricks in a Dry Run

Snap chalk lines on the footing to indicate the perimeter of the wall. Place the bricks on the footing in a dry run, with ³⁄₈- or ¹⁄₂-inch dowels between them to represent the joints. Make sure you understand how the bricks will be laid out at the corners; you may need to cut a brick or two. To minimize cutting, adjust the thickness of the joints or move one wall over an inch or two. With a pencil, mark the footing for the centers of each joint.

2 Lay the First Course

Remove the dry-laid bricks. Starting at a corner, throw a line of mortar for the first three bricks. Set the first brick at the corner, then butter the end of another brick and lay it against the first. As you continue laying bricks, use a level to check that the bricks form an even surface in both directions. Scrape away any excess mortar. Repeat for the second wythe.

3 Lay a Header Course

Where you choose to lay a header course, you may need to cut the corner bricks, as shown. For a common bond, a header course needs two three-quarter bricks and two one-quarter bricks at each corner. To lay a header brick, throw two lines of mortar and set bricks across the two wythes

below. Scrape away excess mortar as you go. Every so often, check the joints to see if they need to be struck (see step 7).

4 Build a Lead

Continue building up the corner only; this is called building a lead. Make a stack seven or eight bricks high. The higher the lead, the longer it must be. As you go, use a level to check that the corner is plumb and that the courses are level. Measure to make sure the joints are the correct thickness. Finally, lay a straightedge diagonally on the corners to see that the bricks form regular "stair steps" at the unfinished end. Do not slide bricks to adjust their position unless you have laid them within the past two minutes. If the mortar has begun to harden and you need to adjust a brick, pick up the brick, scrape off the mortar, and start again.

5 String a Line Between the Leads

Build a lead at the other end of the wall in the same way. Periodically measure to see that the bricks are at the same height as the bricks on the other lead. Hook mason's line blocks and stretch a mason's line from one lead to the other at the center of a joint. The line should be about ⅛ inch from the corners of the bricks. Be sure that the line is taut.

6 Fill In Between Leads

For each course, move the line blocks up one joint and use it as a guide for height and to maintain a straight outer edge. Ensure that no bricks actually touch the line; that would throw it out of alignment. The last brick in the middle of a course, called the closure brick, is buttered at both ends. (If a brick needs to be cut to fit, cut the next-to-last brick and use a full brick for the closure.) Butter generously and slip it in straight down. You may need to use a striking tool to force more mortar into one joint.

7 Strike the Joints

Every 20 minutes or so, depending on weather conditions, test the joints by pressing with your thumb. If a thumbprint holds its shape, it's time to strike. Timing is critical; if the mortar starts to harden, striking will be difficult. Use a jointer to smooth all the horizontal joints, then smooth the verticals. If a bit of mortar

oozes out the side of the jointer, resist the temptation to smear it while it is wet.

8 Clean the Joints and Bricks

As soon as the mortar starts to harden (it will appear crumbly), brush the joints lightly with a masonry brush. If the mortar

smears, stop and wait a few minutes longer. If mortar smears onto the bricks, you may be able to wipe it off with a damp sponge, but take care not to get the joints too wet or you will weaken the mortar. Alternatively, wait a day and then clean with a mild muriatic acid solution.

building with metal framing

Metal framing, also called steel framing, is fire resistant like concrete block but is much lighter. A counter built of metal framing and concrete backerboard will be plenty strong, will withstand freezing winters, and will be light enough to rest on a well-framed deck. Metal framing is also remarkably inexpensive.

Cutting and joining metal framing may feel strange at first if you are used to working with wood, but after an hour or so you will find it an easy material to work with. The metal pieces may feel flimsy by themselves, but they firm up once the backerboard is attached.

With your grill and door specs on hand, make a detailed drawing of the project, including every framing member. Studs and top cross braces should be no more than 16 inches apart. When making your calculations, be sure to include the thickness of the backerboard and your finish stone, tile, or stucco.

1 Measure and Cut the Metal Framing

There are two basic components: U-shaped channels, also called runners, and the studs that fit into the channels. When measuring for cutting a stud, take into account the thickness of the channels—⅛ inch on each end. To make a straight cut, use tin snips on the two sides, then bend the metal back and forth several times to break it. To cut cross braces and other pieces that must have tabs that grab at each end, cut studs 3 inches longer than the opening, then snip each end in two places and bend back two side tabs. This will give you three tabs that can attach to an adjoining channel or stud.

2 Attach the Pieces

Cut and assemble a rectangle of channels to form the bottom of the frame. For some of these channels you will need to cut one or two tabs so you can join them together at the corners. Lay out to see the positions of the studs and double-check your measurements. To attach a stud, slip it into the channel and drive self-tapping screws made specifically for metal studs.

3 Assemble the Frame

The framing will be unstable as you work. As you attach the pieces, check repeatedly for square. First frame the back and the sides. Cut the upper channels, then cut studs to fit between them. Next build the framing in front, which has openings for doors and a barbecue unit. Make cross braces with tabs and screw the tabs into the upper channel.

4 Check the Openings

Set the doors and the cooking units in place to make sure the openings are the correct sizes. When fitting the grill, take into account the thickness of the countertop you have chosen. If the grill needs to be supported from below, see pages 106–107. If the openings are slightly large, you can cut backerboard to overhang the framing by as much as an inch to make a tighter fit. Taking into account the thickness of the backerboard and the finish material, determine how you will attach the doors.

5 Add the Backerboard

When you measure concrete backerboard for cutting, subtract ¼ inch, as the edges tend to be ragged. Use a square or a straightedge to guide your cuts. To make a straight cut, score one side several times with a backerboard knife or a utility knife, snap the piece, and then score the opposite side. To make a cutout, use a reciprocating saw or jigsaw

equipped with a masonry blade. Before you attach the backerboard, check the framing for square. Attach it by driving concrete backerboard screws every 4 inches or so into the studs and the channels. Once all the backerboard is installed, check again that the doors and the cooking units will fit.

building a
wood counter

Decks, overheads, and
other outdoor structures
are made of wood, so
there is no reason you can't build
a counter out of wood as well.
A wood-framed counter will be
light enough to rest on a paver
patio or even a deck, as long as
the countertop is not made of
poured concrete or another extra-
heavy material. The wood should
be covered with a layer of concrete backerboard, which will
protect it from heat. Still, be sure
your grill or any other cooking
unit has an insulating jacket that
makes it warm rather than hot
wherever it touches the counter.

BUILDING TIPS

Build with pressure-treated
lumber, which will survive for a
very long time. If the bottom
of the counter will stay wet for
prolonged periods, use a piece
of composite decking (composed
largely of vinyl) for the bottom
plate. Choose lumber that is
straight and free of cracks. This
project uses 2 by 4s, which are
easily available. You may choose
to build with 2 by 3s instead.

All cuts should be exactly
90 degrees. A power miter box or
a radial-arm saw is recommended,
but you can also use a circular
saw if you are skilled.

1 **Build the Front Wall**
Carefully plan the openings so
the grill and the doors will fit.
Remember that the opening for
the grill will be covered with
$\frac{1}{2}$-inch backerboard, so the wood-
framed opening must be 1 inch
wider and $\frac{1}{2}$-inch deeper than
the finished opening. If you are
using outdoor kitchen doors, make
sure there is enough clearance
for their flanges. This counter is
34 inches tall, meaning it will
be 36 inches tall once a 2-inch-
thick countertop is installed.
That means the studs (vertical
pieces) are 31 inches long.

Cut the bottom plate to the
length of the counter, minus
1 inch for the thickness of the
backerboard on each end. Cut
the top plates to the desired
lengths and cut a
number of studs to
31 inches. Assemble
the frame on a large
flat surface. Lay
the top and bottom
plates next to each
other and mark
for the locations of
the studs. Set all
the pieces in place
and use a framing
square to check the
corners. Drive two
3-inch deck screws
into each joint.

2 Assemble the Four Sides

Build the sidewalls and the rear wall in the same way as you built the front wall. These will be much more straightforward. Working with a helper, hold two or more walls in position. Check the corners for square and make sure the tops are flush with each other. Connect the walls by driving several deck screws at each corner.

3 Add the Top Braces

Cut braces to the same length as the plates of the sidewalls. Position two braces on each side of the sink, if there will be one, and space the others no farther than 16 inches apart. To attach a brace, hold it flush with the top plate, drill an angled pilot hole on each side, and drive 3-inch screws.

4 Add a Plywood Floor

Use ³/₄-inch pressure-treated plywood for the floor. Cut the pieces to fit snugly. You will need to cut notches where the plywood goes around the studs. Attach the plywood by driving 2-inch deck screws every 8 inches or so.

5 Cover with Backerboard

Cut pieces of backerboard to fit (see page 123, step 5) and attach them to the sides of the counter using 2-inch backerboard screws. Also apply backerboard to the top. To make a firm substrate for a tile countertop, spread a layer of thinset mortar on top of the first backerboard layer and add a second layer of backerboard.

finishing a counter with stucco

Stucco is a durable masonry finish that is often applied to the sides of a counter. It may be richly textured or applied nearly smooth. Left uncolored, stucco has a soft, mellow appearance. It can also be tinted before you apply it or painted after it has dried.

This page shows how to stucco a block wall. If you want to cover concrete backerboard, first apply stucco molding, which is made of wire mesh, to the corners.

It will take a couple of hours to get the hang of stuccoing. Fortunately, the base coat, which you apply at the beginning of your learning curve, will be covered up. Before applying the finish coat, practice on a vertical piece of plywood or on an obscure portion of the wall. That way, when you start applying the final coat to a visible area, you will be practiced enough to produce a consistent-looking surface.

1 Apply the Base Coat

Coat the counter wall with latex bonding agent. Pour half a bag of dry stucco base-coat mix into a wheelbarrow or mixing trough. Add water and mix with a mason's hoe or a garden hoe to produce a pasty consistency. The stucco should be just firm enough to hold its shape when you pick it up with a trowel.

Place a shovelful of stucco on a mason's hawk, as shown, or on a piece of plywood. Hold the hawk against the wall as you work so that you can catch any drips. Scoop up the stucco with a straight finishing trowel and spread it upward onto the wall, all the time pressing it into place. Aim for a coat that has a uniform thickness of ½ inch.

2 Scarify the Base Coat

The base coat is also called the scratch coat because it gets roughed up with grooves to ensure that the next coat will stick. Before the stucco starts to harden, comb the surface with a scarifying tool. You can make one by driving 4-penny nails through a piece of 2 by 2 at 1-inch intervals. Work to produce grooves without raising large crumbs.

Once the base coat has hardened but before it dries, spray it with a fine mist of water. The slower the stucco cures, the stronger it will be. Spray it every few hours (more often if it is in the sun) over two days.

or four directions. Brush while the stucco is still wet. If the brush starts to leave globs, rinse it off and keep going.

- To make a spatter coat, dip a whisk broom into the stucco and shake it toward the wall. Aim for a pattern that evenly distributes large and small globs. It may help to add a bit of water to the stucco that gets spattered.

- To make a knockdown texture, first spatter the wall or push a trowel flat onto the stucco and pull it out to form a pattern of peaks. Wait about 15 minutes (depending on the humidity) and then run a trowel very lightly over the surface to flatten some, but not all, of the spatters or peaks. Many people find that a rounded pool trowel, as shown below, is easier to work with than a square-cornered trowel.

3 Apply the Finish Coat

Mix and apply stucco for the finish coat using the same method you used for the base coat, except make the mix slightly wetter. If you buy white stucco finish, you can mix it with dry or liquid colorant for long-lasting color.

When you come to an outside corner, hold a piece of 1 by 4 against the adjoining wall and apply the stucco up to it.

4 Create a Texture

Create the final texture before the stucco starts to dry. To make a swirled texture as shown, set the blade of a masonry trowel in the stucco and rotate it to create half a circle. Make swirls that overlap each other by roughly the same amount. Avoid arcs that appear stacked on top of each other.

OTHER TEXTURES

Professional stucco texturers often develop custom textures that only they can replicate. With practice, you too can create a texture of your own. Here are some possibilities:

- Brush the stucco lightly with a mason's brush. You may choose overlapping rainbowlike swirls, as shown below. Or brush with short strokes that run in three

Brush texture

Spatter texture

Knockdown texture

facing with stone

You can achieve a variety of looks by covering a counter with stone. Choose among facing stones that are random in shape for a jigsaw appearance, or choose stones that are fully or partially squared off for the look of a stone wall. Thinner and lighter stones, often labeled "veneer stone," will be easier to install than flagstones designed for patio flooring. Faux stone (see opposite page) is the easiest of all. If you choose to install very thick stones, they must be stacked on top of each other much as if you were building a stone wall, and they should be tied to the wall with corrugated metal strips (see pages 53–54). Stone can be applied to a block wall or to concrete backerboard.

1 Make a Dry Run

Lay a sheet of plywood, as wide as the counter is tall, on the ground right next to the counter wall you will cover. Lay the stones on the plywood as they will appear on the wall. Play around with the arrangement, making cuts as necessary, until you achieve a pleasing pattern with joints that are fairly consistent in width.

2 Skim Coat the Wall

Dampen the wall by misting it with water. Mix a batch of type S or N mortar (see pages 112–113). The mortar should be fairly stiff—just wet enough to stick to the wall. Use a straight trowel to smear the mortar onto the wall, pressing it into the wall as you work. Aim for a coat about $\frac{3}{8}$ inch thick. Cover an area about 5 feet long.

3 Set the Lower Stones

Remove the stones one at a time from the plywood and transfer them to the wall in the same arrangement. Starting at the bottom, press the stones into the mortar. They should feel well stuck when you try to pull them out. If a stone is not well embedded, pull it off and butter its back (see step 4). Use blocks of wood or small rocks to hold the stones in position. Make all adjustments as soon as possible. Avoid moving a stone after the mortar has begun to harden.

4 Set the Upper Stones

Continue setting stones up to the top of the wall. However, if the stones are very heavy and cause the lower stones to slide down, wait for the mortar to set for the lower stones before you install the upper ones. Back-butter the stones as necessary. Clean away any mortar spills immediately.

5 Fill the Joints

After the mortar has hardened, go back and fill the joints with mortar. A mortar bag is a handy tool for this, but some people find it easier to use a small pointed trowel instead. Once the mortar is stiff enough to hold a thumbprint (but before it dries), use a piece of wood or a metal striking tool to tool the mortar to a fairly consistent depth.

FAUX STONE

Faux stone veneer is lightweight, easy to cut, and quick to install. Many types are almost impossible to distinguish from real stone. Because the veneer is light, manufacturers often recommend that you start at the top rather than the bottom. The stones typically are self-spacing, meaning you just butt them against each other to achieve consistent joints. Special pieces wrap around corners to give the appearance of much thicker stone. Some manufacturers recommend that you apply mortar to the back of the stones only, not to the wall.

facing with tile

A block or backerboard-clad counter can be covered with tile. Stone tile is the usual choice because it has a natural appearance and the tiles are large, but you can install ceramic tile as well. Vertical counter tiles do not need to be as cleanable as countertop tiles, because they will not get handled much, but be sure to choose tiles that will survive in your climate. Most stone tile will be durable as long as you brush on acrylic sealer every couple of years.

1 Lay Out and Cut Tiles to Fit

Most stone tiles are 12 inches square, which makes it easy to lay out the job. Plan the installation so you will not end up with narrow slivers at any point. It sometimes looks best to install narrow tiles under the grill or above a door, where they will be less visible. Note that on two of the walls, tiles will need to run past the block or backerboard by ½ inch or so to cover the ends of the tiles on the adjoining walls.

You can make straight cuts in ceramic tile using a snap cutter (see page 133, step 5), but you will need a wet-cutting masonry saw to cut stone tile or to make a cutout in ceramic tile. Rent a wet saw or buy an inexpensive model. Cutting is easy. Just make sure that water is spraying on the blade at all times. If the saw cuts dry for even a few seconds, the blade may dull.

2 Seal Stone Tiles

Porous stone tiles should be sealed before they are installed, or after they have been installed but before they have been grouted. Otherwise, grout will soak into the stone and present a difficult cleaning problem or even a permanent stain. Brush acrylic masonry sealer on the side of the tile that will be visible. Work carefully and avoid getting sealer on the edges.

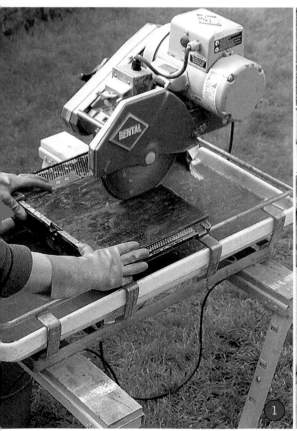

3 Trowel Thinset

In a bucket, use a margin trowel to mix a batch of thinset mortar that is fortified with liquid latex or powdered polymer. Mix to the consistency of mayonnaise, allow the mixture to slake for ten minutes or so, and stir again. If the mixture is too stiff to stick to the counter, you can add a bit of liquid at this point. If it becomes stiff or crumbly later on, throw the batch out and mix another. Scoop the thinset out of the bucket onto a trowel with square notches of the size recommended by your tile dealer (1/4-inch by 1/4-inch is common). Spread first using the flat side of the trowel, pressing the mortar into the counter as you go. Then use the notched side of the trowel to spread the mortar to a consistent depth. The teeth of the trowel should just barely scrape the counter as you work.

4 Set the Tiles

Press the tiles into the mortar. Occasionally pull a tile out to check that at least 80 percent of its back is covered with mortar. You may need to scrape a thin layer of mortar onto the back of each tile. Make sure the bottom row of tiles is level and at a consistent distance from the top of the counter. Use plastic spacers to maintain consistent grout lines. Where a tile is not held in place by a tile below, use pieces of tape to hold it in place until the mortar sets.

5 Grout

Allow the mortar to cure for a day or two and then pry out the plastic spacers. Mix a batch of latex- or polymer-fortified grout and apply it using a laminated grout float. First hold the float nearly flat and press the grout into the joints. Then tilt the float up and use it like a squeegee to scrape away most of the thinset. Run the float in several directions to be sure the joints are filled.

6 Wipe the Surface and Tool the Joints

Use a damp sponge to wipe the surface and to tool the joints to a consistent depth. Wipe several times, allow the grout to dry, then buff the surface with a dry cloth. If you end up with a grout haze on the tiles, wait a day or so and clean it using vinegar or a mild muriatic acid solution.

tiling a countertop

Glazed ceramic tile is the usual choice for a countertop because it is easy to keep clean. Stone tiles can also work well as long as you keep them protected with acrylic masonry sealer. Buy tiles that will survive in your climate.

Countertop tiles must be strong. Do not use soft wall tiles, which will almost certainly crack over time. Unless you don't mind seeing the rough edges of field tiles, you will need to purchase special tiles for the edges. The installation shown here uses V-cap at the edges, but you can also use bullnose pieces, which have one rounded edge, with an edging piece placed just below the bullnose. Whichever arrangement you choose, make sure you have the pieces you need to finish all your edges and corners.

Note that V-cap typically has a raised corner designed to keep water from flowing off the countertop. That is not practical outdoors, where you want to avoid pools of rainwater. The solution is to install the V-cap upside down so that water can run off the countertop.

Tile can also be set on a concrete substrate (see pages 136–139).

1 Set the Backerboard Substrate

Backerboard should be supported every 16 inches, perhaps with metal studs that span the counter. Use a backerboard knife to cut pieces of ½-inch concrete backerboard. Either have the countertop overhang the counter by an inch or two or just bring it flush to the edge of the counter. Cut holes for the cooking units and

sink and test to see that the units will fit. Spread thinset mortar on top of the counter and set the backerboard in the mortar. Cut a second layer of backerboard pieces, with the joints offset from those of the bottom layer by at least a foot. Use a square-notched trowel to spread thinset mortar on the bottom layer, then set the top layer in the mortar.

2 Prepare the Substrate

Cut and press strips of fiberglass mesh reinforcing tape to fit over the joints and to wrap around the edges. Mix a small batch of thinset mortar and spread it over the tape using the flat side of a trowel. This mortar should be just thick enough to hold the tape in place. Also use the thinset to fill any gaps between backerboard sheets.

3 Make Layout Lines

In both directions at each corner, hold a V-cap piece in place and trace its edge with a pencil. Snap chalk lines running between the trace lines. This marks the outside edge of the field tiles. (When you install the V-cap, mortar along the edge of the backerboard will hold it back from this line by the width of a grout line.)

4 Make a Dry Run

Attach long, straight pieces of wood as battens to temporarily mark the outside edges of the field tiles. Strips of plywood work well for this (factory-cut edges are perfectly straight). Lay the field tiles out in a dry run with plastic spacers. You will likely need to adjust the layout in order to avoid having narrow tiles along one or more edges. Lay all the full tiles in place, then make the cuts.

5 Cut Tiles

Most ceramic tiles can be straight-cut using a snap cutter. Set a tile firmly against the cutter's guide so the cut will be square. Push or pull the cutter all the way across in a single continuous stroke. Place the wings of the cutter on each side of the score and push down to snap the tile. To make a cutout that does not have to be precise (for example, under a sink), you can use a tile nibbling tool. For precise cutouts, or to cut stone tile, use a wet-cutting masonry saw (see page 130, step 1).

6 Lay Out and Cut Corner Pieces

At an inside or outside corner, you may need to cut the V-cap at a 45-degree angle. If you want the V-cap's grout lines to line up with those of the field tiles, you will also need to cut the V-caps to length. Hold them in place with plastic spacers to mark the cut. You'll need a wet-cutting masonry saw to cut the V-cap.

7 Trowel the Thinset

Pick up the dry-laid tiles from a section 3 or 4 feet long and set them aside so you can easily replace them in the correct arrangement. Mix a batch of latex- or polymer-reinforced thinset mortar. Spread it onto the backerboard using a square-notched trowel. Aim for an even surface with few mortar globs.

8 Set the Field Tiles

Starting at a corner where two battens meet, begin setting tiles. Use plastic spacers to maintain even joints. Press each tile into place. Try to set the tiles straight down to avoid sliding a tile more than ½ inch or so. Once you have finished with one 3- to 4-foot-long section, move on to the next.

9 Maintain Straight Lines and Bed the Tiles

Use a straightedge or the flat side of a long trowel to keep the lines straight. Every few minutes pick up a tile and examine its back to make sure the mortar is covering at least 80 percent of its surface. You may need to tap each tile with a straight piece of wood and a mallet, or you may need to apply a thin layer of mortar to the backs of the tiles.

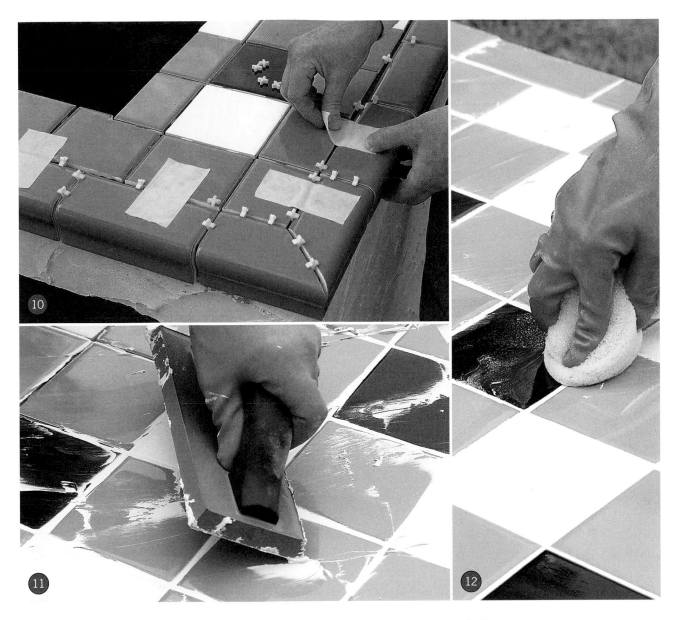

10 Set the V-Caps

Once all the field tiles are set, remove the battens and set the V-caps. Apply mortar to the top of the countertop and to the edges. You may need to apply mortar to the V-caps as well. Use plastic spacers to maintain consistent grout lines. To keep the V-caps in place until the mortar sets, use tape.

11 Apply Grout

Allow the mortar to set for a day or two. Mix a batch of latex-reinforced grout and apply it using a laminated grout float. First press the grout into the joints with the float held nearly flat, moving the float in several directions. Then use the float to scrape away most of the excess mortar. Hold the float at an angle to the joints so it does not dig into them.

12 Wipe and Tool

Use a large sponge to wipe away the excess mortar and to tool the joints to a consistent depth. Take the time to tool each joint. You will need to rinse the sponge often and wipe several times. After the grout has dried, buff the surface with a dry cloth.

forming a concrete countertop

Professionals who specialize in decorative concrete countertops use a variety of techniques to produce surfaces that are one-of-a-kind works of art. Some build elaborate forms, pour the countertop upside down, and flip it over for installation. Often shards of glass or other decorative elements are incorporated. Many installers grind and polish the top after it has cured to produce a silky-smooth finish.

The pour-in-place countertop shown on the following four pages is easier to make, and it still allows you a range of decorative possibilities. You can choose among various concrete colorants, which you can add in any amount to produce a light or dark color. Another approach is to pour a plain gray countertop, allow it to cure, and then apply acid stain. You may also embed decorative pieces, though this may make the surface a bit bumpy.

To support the top, build the counter and install one or two layers of concrete backerboard as a substrate. The backerboard should not overhang the counter. Where the backerboard spans more than 12 inches, support it temporarily by propping 2 by 4s underneath.

You can use the same techniques to build a concrete substrate for a tiled countertop.

KEEPING IT FROM CRACKING

Concrete countertops sometimes crack. Hairline cracks are not a problem and are often seen as added character. However, you should aim to minimize cracking.

- Purchase high-strength concrete. For a small job like a countertop, use bags of concrete mix rated for loads of 5000 pounds per square inch.
- Make a very stiff mix. The thinner the mix, the more likely it is to crack, so add only as much water as is necessary.
- Use metal reinforcement. It will not stop tiny cracks, but it will keep small cracks from getting bigger.
- Add fiber reinforcement, available from a concrete supplier. The fibers stop small cracks, but they can produce small imperfections when you finish the surface. So add fibers to the first part of the pour only.

1 Build the Form

Where you want the countertop to overhang the counter by 1½ inches, cut 2 by 4s to fit snugly and fasten them together as you wrap them around the counter. You may need to hold them up with propped pieces of lumber, and you may need to attach some of them temporarily to the counter using masonry screws. Do not put these pieces around the grill opening or wherever else you do not want the countertop to overhang. Next, cut and attach pieces of 2 by 6 for the main form. The top of the 2 by 6 here is 2½ inches above the backerboard; the total countertop thickness, including the thickness of the backerboard, is 3 inches. Where needed, use a clamp or two to hold the form firmly together.

2 Cut Reinforcing Metal and Seal the Form

To reinforce a small slab like a countertop, stucco lath (as shown) is a good choice. Cut it to fit about an inch from the perimeter of the form. Do not oil the form, because the oil can change the color of the concrete. Apply silicone caulk to seal any gaps so that liquid concrete cannot leak out. At the corners, apply a bead of caulk to help round the edges.

3 Mix the Concrete

Experiment with concrete colors until you achieve a mix you like. Allow the concrete to dry fully and then apply masonry sealer to see the final color. Develop a precise recipe, using a bathroom scale or measuring cup to ensure that you add the same amount of colorant to each batch of concrete. Take care to mix as dry as possible; the concrete should be completely wet but not pourable. To strengthen the concrete, add fiber reinforcement.

4 Pour and Spread the First Layer

Temporarily remove the metal reinforcement and wipe the backerboard with a wet rag to ensure good adhesion. Shovel the concrete into a bucket, then pour from the bucket into the center of the formed area. Starting in the middle and working outward, use a magnesium or Teflon float to spread the concrete so that it is about half the thickness of the countertop. Press down as you spread to ensure that the concrete sticks to the backerboard.

5 Set the Reinforcement and Spread the Top Layer

Set the reinforcing metal on top of the concrete. Add more concrete and spread, pushing down to prevent voids and bubbles. If the form bulges outward as you work, straighten it with bar clamps set across the boards. Continue spreading until the form is full. Set a piece of 2 by 4 on top of the form boards, spanning the form, and screed the top so that it is level with the tops of the form boards.

6 Eliminate Bubbles at the Edges

To minimize air pockets that often occur where the concrete meets the form boards, slip a mason's trowel down between the boards and the concrete and move it along the perimeter using slicing motions. Then tap the sides of the form with a hammer.

7 Float the Concrete

As soon as any bleed water on top of the concrete disappears, run a magnesium or Teflon float across the surface to begin smoothing. Press just hard enough to bring up a little bleed water, then stop floating. If you continue floating while bleed water is present, the surface will weaken and could flake off later.

8 Use an Edger

Run a concrete edger along the perimeter two or three times until the surface is smooth. Again, avoid working the surface when bleed water is present. As soon as the water disappears, run a magnesium or Teflon float over the surface to smooth the resulting ridge.

9 Strip the Form

When the concrete seems hard enough to hold its shape, carefully release the squeeze clamps. If the form bulges outward, tighten the clamps again, wait another 10 minutes or so, and try again. Once all the clamps are off, unscrew the form boards and gently pull them away.

10 Smooth the Edge

If removing the form reveals a pleasingly rocky appearance on the slab's edge, you may choose to leave it like that. To smooth the edge, use a magnesium float, then a steel trowel. If any bubbles are visible, fill them by hand and trowel again.

11 Smooth the Corners

Use a float or trowel to roughly achieve the rounded edge you desire. Then use a small piece of plastic to finish the rounding and smoothing.

12 Finish with a Trowel

Go over the surface with a steel trowel. A pool trowel like the one shown is easier for beginners. Avoid overworking the surface. If troweling starts to roughen rather than smooth, it is time to stop. Cover the countertop with plastic to keep the concrete wet so it can cure slowly over a few days. Once it is fully dry, apply two coats of acrylic masonry sealer or wax.

gas and propane hookups

For a discussion of the pros and cons of natural gas and propane, see pages 28–29. It was once common to buy parts for converting from propane to gas or vice versa, but such a conversion is now against code in many locales, and in other areas it must be performed by a licensed plumber. Make sure the grill you purchase is made for the fuel you have chosen. Plan before you install a gas or propane unit onto the countertop (see pages 148–149), and make most of the natural gas connections or arrange for storage of the propane tanks. Consult your owner's manual to find out if you need to buy any parts, and check that the hose will be long enough.

PROPANE CONNECTIONS

Buy two propane tanks and keep one stored safely away from any source of flame, such as in another compartment of the counter. Keep the extra tank filled so you will lose no cooking time when the first tank runs out.

A typical connection includes a regulator, which ensures that the grill will receive the right amount of propane, as well as a fitting and a rubber hose. If you have two propane cooking units, purchase a setup like the one shown above right. Most fittings are designed to be connected by hand only; do not use pliers or other tools. Making the connec-

HOOKUP FOR A MULTIBURNER GRILL PLUS A SIDE BURNER

SIDE BURNER VALVE

RUBBER HOSE

MULTIPLE BURNER CONTROL VALVES

REGULATOR

tion is easy, but it must be done with care. Make sure the fitting's nipple is centered in the hole in the tank's valve, and hold the fitting straight as you screw it in. If you encounter resistance within the first full turn, you are likely going in at an angle. The result will be cross-threading, which will cause leaks. Unscrew the fitting and try again.

Check for leaks whenever you hook up a tank. Professional plumbers use a special gas testing fluid, which you can purchase. Or, mix a solution of one part water to one part dishwashing soap. Open the tank's valve, and spread the fluid or the soapy water onto the areas shown below. If you see growing bubbles where the fitting meets the tank's valve, shut off the valve and try retightening the fitting. If you see growing bubbles on the tank itself, call your propane gas supplier or the fire department.

WHERE TO TEST FOR LEAKS

BRUSH SOAPY WATER ON THESE POINTS

BRUSH SOAPY WATER ON THESE POINTS

NATURAL GAS CONNECTIONS

Even if you hire a pro to run a gas line from the house (see page 108), you may choose to install the valves and fittings inside the cabinet yourself. Learn local codes for gas connections and follow them scrupulously.

Be sure the gas is shut off at the meter before making any connections or working on gas piping. Codes may require a separate shutoff valve for each gas unit. A length of pipe extending downward a foot or so, called a drip leg, is often required at each valve. To install two valves with drip legs, you will need to use a variety of fittings, as shown below. If you are using solid steel gas pipe (which may be green or black), wrap the male threads with yellow Teflon tape, which is made for gas pipe, before making each connection. Tighten each fitting in turn using a pipe wrench. Be sure to install a regulator (which usually comes with the grill) on the line between the shutoff valve and the grill.

When all the connections are secure, turn the gas back on—but leave the burners off—and check for leaks. Use the soapy-water test shown on the previous page. Also turn off all gas appliances in the house and check your meter. If it shows any sign of movement after five minutes or so, recheck for leaks using soapy water.

DUAL GAS VALVES

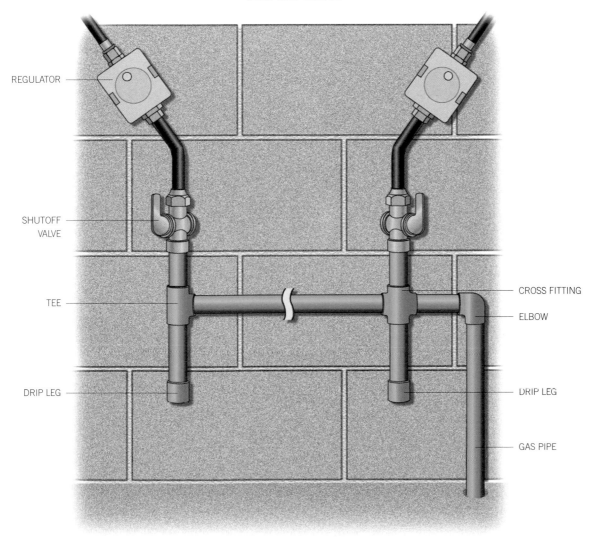

REGULATOR

SHUTOFF VALVE

TEE

DRIP LEG

CROSS FITTING

ELBOW

DRIP LEG

GAS PIPE

electrical connections

Electrical receptacles are necessary for small appliances, rotisseries, charcoal starters, refrigerators, and for countertop appliances like blenders and food processors. Make sure the appliances you use will not overload a circuit, and be sure to follow local codes when you run conduit or cable to the inside of the counter (see pages 108–109). Even if you hire a pro to run the main line, you may choose to install the individual receptacles and lights yourself.

Once you have a single conduit inside the counter, you can install a number of receptacles or light fixtures. (However, running conduit through a block wall to the outside of the counter is best accomplished before you install the countertop; see page 117, step 11.) For complete instructions on making electrical connections and installing boxes, see Sunset's *Complete Home Wiring.* Some of the most common connections are shown here.

1 Install Branch Lines
PVC conduit is the most common way to run exposed outdoor wiring, but check with your building department to see if it requires another material, such as metal. To install a fitting with branch lines, cut all the pipes (using a PVC saw, hacksaw, or hand saw) to the desired lengths and assemble the pipes and fit-

tings in a complete dry run. Once you are satisfied with the arrangement, draw layout lines on the fittings and pipes to indicate how they should fit together. This is necessary for some but not all joints. Disassemble the pieces and keep them in order. In most cases, you do not need to apply primer to the joints before applying glue, but check with local codes to be sure. Working in order, glue the pieces one at a time. Apply PVC cement to the inside of the fitting and the end of the pipe, then immediately insert the pipe into the fitting, give a slight twist, and hold for 15 seconds or so.

2 Pull Wires
Once the conduit has been glued together, anchor it to the walls every 16 inches or so using pipe straps and masonry screws. To pull wires through the pipes, insert the end of a fish tape into a box or a fitting with a removable cover, called a pulling fitting, and push it all the way to the other end, at the house. Wrap the wires (usually there are three: a black hot wire, a white neutral wire, and a bare ground wire) around the end of the fish tape and secure them with electrician's tape. Turn the fish tape's crank to reel in the wires.

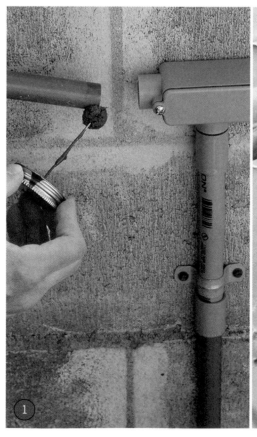

3 Connect a Receptacle

Ground-fault circuit interrupter receptacles (GFCIs) are usually required for outdoor installations. To hook one up, make sure that the power is shut off at the circuit panel. Use wire strippers to remove about 1 inch of insulation from the ends of the black and white wires. Bend the exposed wire ends in a loop. Hook the black wire around the brass terminal screw marked LINE, then tighten the screw. Connect the white wire in the same way to the silver screw marked LINE. If you want to run wires that bring power from this receptacle to others, hook those wires to the terminals marked LOAD. (Note that any receptacles that are extensions of a GFCI receptacle will be GFCI protected even if they are non-GFCI receptacles. The same holds true for any lights or appliances wired in the same way.)

4 Add an In-Use Cover

If the receptacle is inside the counter, you can install a simple cover plate. If the receptacle is exposed, install an in-use cover, which protects the receptacle from rain even when appliances are plugged into it. Install the gaskets carefully so the receptacle will be watertight.

LOW-VOLTAGE LIGHTING

At a home center you will find a wide variety of low-voltage lights that can be attached to the top of a counter, mounted on the side of an overhead, or set into a structure. Installing them is easy. Buy a kit or separate parts including a timer-transformer and enough low-voltage cord to reach your destination. Attach the transformer to a wall near an electrical receptacle, run the cord in a shallow trench to the counter, and anchor the light. Connect the wire to the light and staple the cord where necessary. Connect the cord to the transformer and plug the transformer into the receptacle.

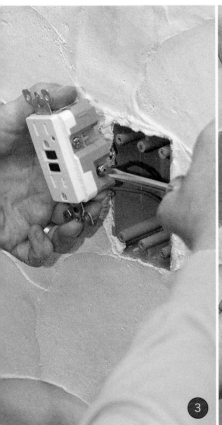

3

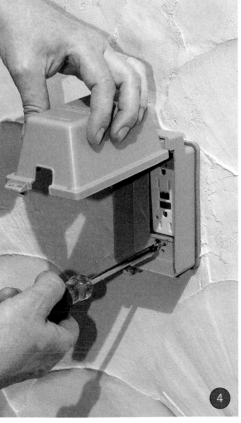

4

plumbing hookups

A sink is often the component that raises a simple barbecue counter to true outdoor kitchen status. Supply lines and the drain line must be run (or "roughed in") before you pour the slab (see pages 108–109). Even if you hire a pro for the rough-in work, you may choose to hook up the sink and faucet yourself.

Check with your building department to see that you are using supply and drainpipes that meet local codes. Supply pipes are often solid copper, but CPVC (a type of rigid plastic pipe) or PEX (a flexible plastic tubing) may be allowed. In some areas, black ABS drainpipe is specified, while in others white PVC is required. To learn basic techniques for cutting and joining these types of pipe, see Sunset's *Complete Home Plumbing*.

Unless the counter is up against the house, it is usually easiest to rough one cold-water supply pipe into the counter area. You can then install an electric on-demand water heater, also called a tankless water heater. Consult with your supplier to make sure the heater will sufficiently heat your water. Some units may not work effectively if the incoming cold water is too cold. This type of heater is easy to install. Simply mount it on the wall, hook the pipes to it (see below), and plug it in. It is efficient, since it turns on only when you need it for your outdoor faucet, and it provides hot water instantly. An outdoor kitchen usually needs only a very small unit, which plugs into a standard 120-volt receptacle and pulls as little as 500 watts. Make sure that the unit you choose will not overload the electrical circuit it is on.

UNDER-COUNTER PLUMBING HOOKUPS

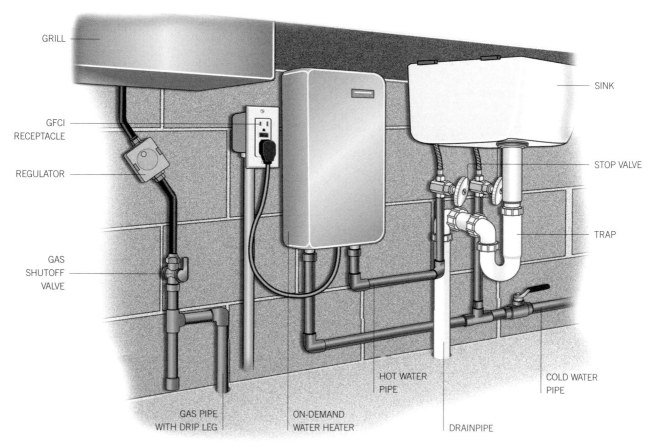

GRILL

GFCI RECEPTACLE

REGULATOR

GAS SHUTOFF VALVE

SINK

STOP VALVE

TRAP

GAS PIPE WITH DRIP LEG

ON-DEMAND WATER HEATER

HOT WATER PIPE

DRAINPIPE

COLD WATER PIPE

1 Install Stop Valves

Plumbing codes call for stop valves, also called fixture shutoff valves, so that you can quickly shut off water running to the faucet. Choose stop valves with inlets that will join to your supply pipes (for example, $\frac{1}{2}$-inch copper) and with receptacles sized to join to your supply tubes (see page 147, step 7).

If you are working with copper pipe, you will need to learn how to solder (or "sweat") the joints, both to install stop valves and to connect any pipe fittings. Cut the pipes to size using a tubing cutter and ream out the inside burrs. Use a wire brush or plumber's sandpaper to polish the last inch of pipe and the inside of the fitting so they shine. Apply soldering flux to the polished surfaces and push the parts together. Direct the flame of a propane torch onto the fitting or valve, not the pipe, and move it around to distribute the heat evenly. Touch the tip of the pipe solder to the joint, and capillary action will suck solder into the joint. When the solder shows all the way around the fitting, wait a few seconds and then carefully wipe the joint with a damp rag.

2 Install a Basket Strainer

Turn the sink upside down on a pair of workhorses so you can easily reach both sides. Disassemble a basket strainer and apply plumber's putty to its flange. From underneath, press the strainer in place and hold it firmly using the handles of a pair of pliers. From above, slip on the rubber washer, the cardboard washer, and the hold-down nut. Tighten the nut using large slip-joint pliers or a spud wrench.

3 Assemble the Trap

Assemble as much of the plumbing as possible before you install the sink; working inside the counter after the sink is installed is cramped and difficult. If codes allow, use a plastic trap with nuts that can be tightened by hand. Otherwise, you will need to tighten the nuts using slip-joint pliers. When assembling a trap, be sure to install the correct washer—which may be plastic or rubber—at each joint. If you want a garbage disposer, now is the time to install it. For a simple single-bowl sink as shown, install a tailpiece onto the strainer, then add the trap piece. If you have a double-bowl sink, install a center-set trap, which connects the drain lines from the two bowls. Set the sink in place temporarily to see if you need to cut the tailpiece in order to line it up with the drainpipe. If you must run a horizontal drain line, make sure it slopes at a rate of at least ¼-inch per foot. Once you are sure of the fit, set the sink back on the horses and tighten the joints.

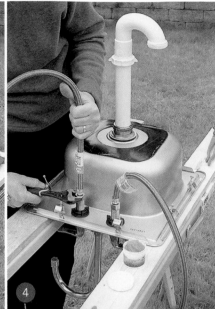

4 Install a Faucet

Single-handle faucets are typically installed with copper inlet tubes running through the center hole. Two-handle faucets typically have inlets that run through both of the side holes, as shown. Follow the manufacturer's directions for anchoring the faucet to the sink. Attach braided supply tubes to the inlets. Tighten firmly, but take care not to twist any faucet parts. Set the sink in place to make sure the supply tubes can reach the stop valves.

5 Set the Sink

Once you are sure all the plumbing will fit, press a generous rope of plumber's putty to the underside of the sink's flange. Slide at least two mounting clips onto each side of the flange and use plumber's putty to hold the clips still while you set the sink. Lower the sink into place, check that it is sealed all the way around, and press it into place. If you have a cast-iron rather than a stainless-steel sink, you will not need to use clips.

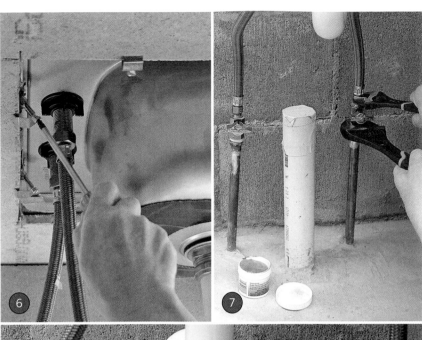

6 Tighten the Mounting Clips

From underneath, position the clips so they grab onto the counter. Tighten the clips using a screwdriver or a drill with a screwdriver bit. From above, check that the sink is sealed all around. Putty should ooze out of the flange at every point. Once the clips are tightened, clean away the excess putty.

7 Connect the Supply Lines

Attach the supply tubes to the stop valves. Hot goes to the left handle, and cold goes to the right handle. Tighten using two wrenches as shown so that you do not kink the faucet's copper tubes as you tighten. Turn off the faucet and turn on the water supply, then check for leaks. Tighten as needed.

8 Connect the Drain Line

Slide on nuts and washers and tighten the nuts to connect the drain line. To test the drain line for leaks, plug the bowl, fill it with water, and pull the plug. Use a flashlight to look for leaks, and feel with your hand. If the pipes are not bone dry, you may need to tighten a nut or two. The S trap arrangement shown is not allowed by some local codes. You may be required to add a 3-inch horizontal piece at the bottom of the S.

installing grills and doors

Once the counter and the countertop are finished, it is time for the crowning touch—adding the cooking appliances and doors. See pages 106–107 for information on planning the grill opening. This is usually not difficult, but it should be done carefully to ensure that the units are firmly attached and well sealed.

KEEPING IT DRY

Many outdoor counters have a problem with rainwater seeping through the gap around a grill or through a door opening to the inside of the counter. You may not be able to keep the counter totally dry during a heavy storm, but if you apply caulk with care, you can keep nearly all the water out. Of course, covering the counter with a tarp during rainfalls will help a great deal.

Silicone caulk is usually the best choice because it stays flexible for many years. However, inexpensive silicones sometimes do not adhere well. To ensure adhesion, buy the highest-quality silicone caulk you can find (it may be labeled "Silicone II") and make sure that the surfaces are completely dry and free of dust before you apply it.

Applying a good bead of caulk does take some skill. Practice on a test area until you can lay down a bead that is smooth and even. If caulk fails to seal, it usually does not help to apply a second bead over the old. Instead, thoroughly scrape away the old caulk and try again.

Standard silicone caulk is generally able to withstand temperatures of up to 400 degrees. Most grill and cooktop bodies do not exceed that temperature, even if they achieve higher cooking temperatures. However, to be safe you can apply high-temperature silicone caulk made for sealing stove flues. You may need to go to a store that specializes in wood-burning stoves to buy this product.

INSTALLING A GRILL OR COOKTOP

1 Set the Grill in Place

Read the manufacturer's directions and make sure all the requisite parts are attached to the grill. Then measure to see that the gas line will reach the shutoff valve. Have another person or two help you lift a heavy grill. Carefully thread the line through the opening as you slide or set the grill in place. Hook it up to a gas line or propane tank, turn on the gas, and test for leaks (see page 140).

mortar or stucco, or cut it away using a circular saw equipped with a masonry blade.

Hold the door in position, flat against the counter's wall, and drill pilot holes for the screws. You may need to angle the holes so that the screws will drive into a solid surface, such as concrete block or stone facing. Remove the door, wipe away any dust, and apply a generous bead of caulk to the door's flange.

2 Install the Door

Press the door in place and make sure that caulk seals the flange at all points. Drive masonry screws into the pilot holes. If you have built the counter using steel or wood framing, drive sheet-metal screws or wood screws instead.

2 Caulk Around a Grill

If there is a gap greater than $\frac{1}{4}$ inch between the grill or cook-top and the countertop, fill it with latex-fortified grout and wait for the grout to dry fully before applying caulk. If a grill or cook-top has a removable or adjustable flange, give yourself double protection. First apply one bead of caulk to seal the gap between the appliance's body and the counter-top. After that has dried, apply a second bead under or around the flange. If the grill's flange is not removable or adjustable, caulk the area around the opening and set the grill on top of the caulk. It is usually a good idea to apply caulk to the front of the grill as well.

3 Sealing a Flange

If possible, apply a bead of caulk under the flange and then lower the flange onto the wet caulk. Also apply a thin bead of caulk where the flange meets the grill. Either carefully wipe the caulk while it is wet or wait for it to dry and clean it away with a knife and scraper.

INSTALLING A DOOR

1 Test Fit, Drill Holes, and Caulk

Set a door in its opening to be sure that it will fit and that the door will open and close. If you have to force a door into a space that is too tight, it might not open and close smoothly. To slightly enlarge an opening, you may need to scrape away excess

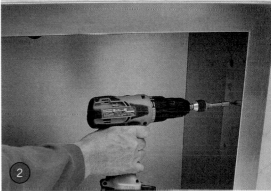

building an overhead

Unless your counter is in a shady area, there's a good chance you will feel the need for an overhead structure for hot summer afternoons. An overhead not only adds comfort, it also frames a kitchen and makes it feel a bit, though not too much, like a room.

Choose a design that harmonizes with your home and yard. An overhead need not be built from the same materials as your house, but any new materials should not create a jarring contrast. A formal setting probably calls for neatly spaced members and several coats of paint. A more informal home may call for an unpainted overhead with a few fanciful elements.

Consider the sight lines from the house and from the patio. Make sure the new overhead will not inhibit a desired view or make an outdoor room too dark. Also plan so the posts won't impede traffic flow. You may be able to move a post to the side by using an angled bracket, or even eliminate a post by tying to a nearby wall (see page 71 for an example of these strategies).

HOW IT'S PUT TOGETHER

An overhead may be freestanding or attached to the house at one end with a ledger. Posts are usually set deep in holes for added lateral strength, but in the case of an attached structure they may rest on post anchors that are attached to a patio. A solid beam, typically made of 4-by lumber, can rest on top of the posts. You can also build a beam using two pieces of 2-by lumber, with one

RAFTER AND BEAM SPANS

If rafters or beams span too long a distance, they will sag in time. Here are some recommended maximum spans. (A rafter span is the distance from beam to beam, or from the beam to the ledger. A beam span is the distance from post to post.)

RAFTER SIZE	IF RAFTERS ARE SPACED	
	16" APART	24" APART
2 × 4	9'	8'
2 × 6	14'	12'
2 × 8	18'	16'

BEAM SIZE	IF BEAMS ARE SPACED	
	12' APART	16' APART
2 × 8	8'	6'
2 × 10	10'	8'
4 × 6	8'	6'
4 × 8	12'	10'
4 × 10	14'	12'

Note: A doubled 2-by beam has the same strength as a 4-by beam. For instance, a beam made with two 2 × 6s is equivalent to one 4 × 6.

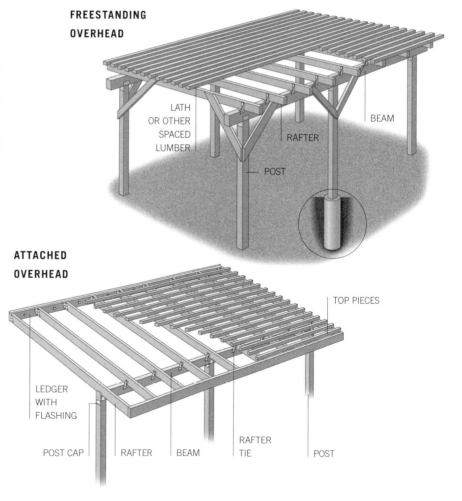

FREESTANDING OVERHEAD

LATH OR OTHER SPACED LUMBER

BEAM

RAFTER

POST

ATTACHED OVERHEAD

TOP PIECES

LEDGER WITH FLASHING

POST CAP   RAFTER   BEAM   RAFTER TIE   POST

attached to each side of the post (below). With this type of beam, you can install 4-by-4 bracing as shown. Rafters rest on top of two beams, or they may tie into a ledger at one end.

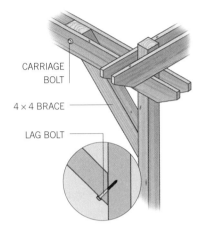

CARRIAGE BOLT

4 × 4 BRACE

LAG BOLT

Top pieces, sometimes called lath, are usually evenly spaced and sized to provide the right amount of shade. These pieces are commonly 1 by 2s, 2 by 2s, or other small-dimension lumber. But there are other options. Shade cloths are available in a variety of densities to provide from 20 to 90 percent shade. Lattice panels install quickly, provide fairly even shade throughout the day, and add a richly textured look. Be sure to support the lattice every 16 inches or it will sag. Other options include woven reeds or bamboo, which can be rolled up when shade is not desired.

Use lumber that will resist rotting and warping. Pressure-treated lumber is the most rot resistant; the dark heartwood of redwood or cedar also resists rot and is a better looking choice for a landscape structure.

SHADE STRATEGIES

Shade needs vary throughout the day and during the year, so spend some time developing a plan. If you want midday shade, run the top pieces east to west. For more shade in the morning and early evening, run the pieces north to south. Keep in mind that changing the orientation of the top pieces means changing the orientation of the beams and rafters as well.

Experiment with different materials and configurations by temporarily screwing some pieces on top of the rafters. Pay attention to the amount of shade they provide in both the morning and afternoon. Top pieces laid on edge diffuse early-morning and late-afternoon sun but let in plenty of light at midday (below, top). The same pieces laid flat (below, bottom) admit more sun

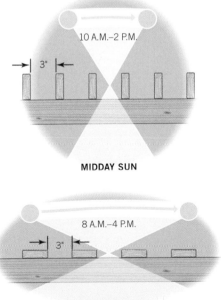

10 A.M.–2 P.M.

3"

MIDDAY SUN

8 A.M.–4 P.M.

3"

EARLY-MORNING AND LATE-AFTERNOON SUN

in the early morning and late afternoon but block midday sun.

RAFTER AND BEAM ENDS

Overhanging rafter and beam ends are highly visible, so you may want to cut them to achieve a decorative pattern. Some examples are shown here. Experiment

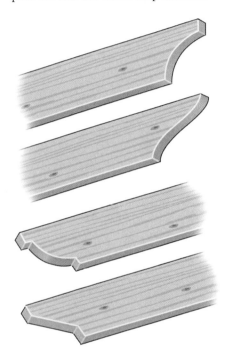

with designs, using a compass if the design calls for a curve or two. Once you've settled on a pleasing look, make a cardboard or plywood template and use it to trace the pattern onto the rafter or beam ends. To make the cuts, you will likely need to use a jigsaw in addition to a circular saw.

You can also dress up post tops. The easiest way is to buy decorative post caps that screw in. Or use a circular saw to cut a series of shallow bands and perhaps to make chamfer cuts all around the tops.

ATTACHING A LEDGER

If the overhead will be attached to the house, begin construction by installing a ledger. The ledger is typically made of the same dimension lumber as the rafters. A ledger must be firmly attached with long screws that reach into the house's framing—not just the siding and sheathing. On a one-story house, it is often best to attach the ledger just below the eaves. On a two-story house, you can usually tie into a band joist (also called a rim joist) between the floors. You can find the band joist by measuring down from a second-story window; the top of the joist is usually about $1\frac{1}{2}$ inches below the floor surface.

The method of attachment varies depending on the type of siding and local building codes. Avoid creating a joint where water will collect and cause rot. Some builders prefer to cut out a section of siding, slip in metal flashing, and tuck the ledger under the flashing. However, simpler arrangements work just as well. If you have beveled horizontal siding, use an inverted piece of siding (shown above) to create a plumb surface for attaching the ledger. If your siding is not beveled, you may simply screw the ledger tight to it or use the holdback method (shown above, inset). Slip three or four stainless-steel washers between the ledger and the siding when driving each screw. This will allow water to flow behind the

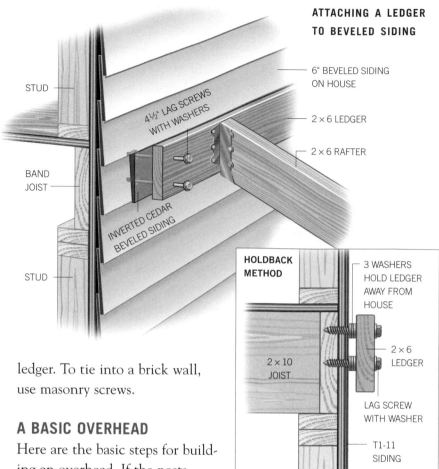

ledger. To tie into a brick wall, use masonry screws.

A BASIC OVERHEAD

Here are the basic steps for building an overhead. If the posts will sit on top of a patio that is reasonably level or consistently sloped, cut all the posts to the same length. Otherwise, install the posts longer than necessary and then cut them to a uniform height later in the process.

1 Set the Posts

Lay out for post locations so that the overhead will have square corners. Dig post holes at least 2 feet deep. If there is an existing patio made of pavers laid in sand, you can remove some pavers to dig the holes (you'll need to cut pavers to fit around the posts later). If possible, dig postholes just beyond the patio. If you have

a concrete patio, you may choose to set the posts on top using post anchors that elevate them slightly. To install an anchor, drill holes using a masonry bit and drive masonry screws.

Plumb each post in both directions; a post level makes this easy. Secure each post with temporary wood braces nailed to wood stakes driven into the ground or to heavy weights resting on the patio. You may fill the postholes with concrete or well-tamped soil at this point, or you may wait until the entire structure is built before doing so. Use a level set atop a long, straight board to mark all the posts for cutting at the same height.

2 Install the Beams

If you have a ledger, the top of the beam should be at the same height as the bottom of the ledger. A beam should overhang the posts by at least a few inches on each side. To install a solid beam on top of the posts, work with two or more helpers. Attach a post cap to the top of each post, slip the beam into the caps, and drive deck screws or nails to attach it. If you do not like the appearance of a post cap, set the beam directly on top of the post, drill angled pilot holes, and drive screws to attach the beam to the post.

To install a beam made of two pieces, as shown on page 151, use a square to draw lines around the post to mark the exact height of the beam on both sides. Attach the two pieces using deck screws or nails, or drill holes and drive bolts through all three pieces.

3 Add Rafters and Braces

On top of the beams and/or on the side of the ledger, mark for evenly spaced rafters. Cut rafters to overhang the beams by at least a few inches. Attach the rafters by drilling angled pilot holes and driving screws or nails, or use a rafter tie, as shown. To make the structure more stable, nail or screw 2-by-4 or 2-by-6 braces between the beams and posts. The braces should be at least 3 feet long, with the ends cut at 45 degrees.

4 Add Top Pieces

Top the structure with 1 by 2s or other small-dimension lumber spaced to achieve the desired amount of shade (see page 151). One method, called self-spacing, is to use a scrap of the same lumber as a guide for spacing.

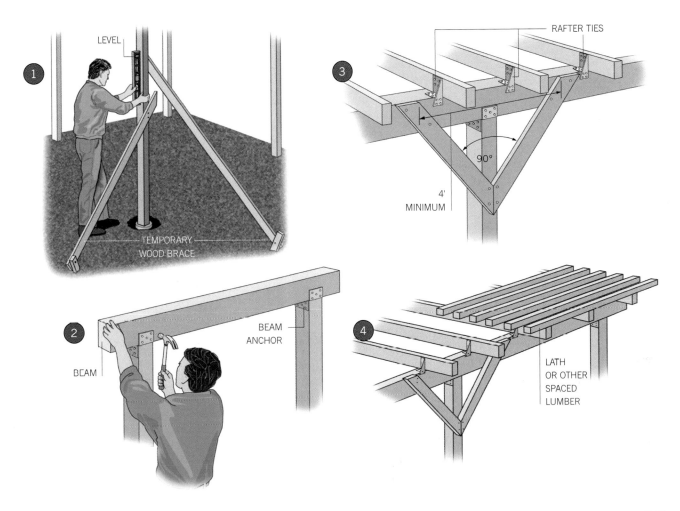

grilling tips

Whether you cook with charcoal or gas, grilling over an open fire makes possible a variety of smoky flavors and aromas, as well as crunchy or soft textures. Here are some ideas to get you started on creating your own repertoire of recipes and techniques.

THE RIGHT HEAT

As a general rule, cook thin pieces of meat quickly over high heat to sear the outside and keep the inside juicy. Cook larger pieces at a lower temperature. You may choose to first sear a roast or bird quickly at high temperature, then reduce the heat for slow cooking.

OVEN TEMPERATURE If your grill has a thermometer mounted in the center of the lid, you can quickly tell how hot the air inside the grill is. High heat is 450°F to 550°F, medium heat is 350°F to 450°F, and low heat is 250°F to 350°F. These temperature readings are useful when you are roasting something large like a whole fish, roast, or chicken.

GRATE TEMPERATURE If you are grilling thin items like steak or vegetables, the thermometer will not be much help, as it does not tell how hot the grate is. To test for grilling temperature, use the hand test: Hold your hand four to five inches above the grate and count "one alligator, two alligator." If you need to remove your hand after two or three alligators, you have high heat. If you need to remove your hand sooner, it's probably too hot for cooking. Four to five alligators is medium-high heat, six to eight alligators is medium heat, and nine to ten alligators is medium-low heat.

ADDING OUTDOORSY FLAVORS

There are a good variety of wood chips made for barbecuing, including hickory, mesquite, apple, and cherry. Alternatively, you can simply place a small hardwood log on top of the coals. Soak a log or wood chips in water for about 20 minutes before putting them on a fire.

Many gas grills come with a smoker box, to which you can add wood chips. If you do not have one, wrap a handful of wood chips firmly in a pouch of aluminum foil, then poke holes in the top. Place the pouch under the grate directly over one of the burners. Run the grill on high until you see smoke coming out of the holes, then lower the flame to the cooking temperature.

A dry rub is a combination of seasonings applied to meat soon before cooking. The meat, which is moist, causes the rub to become moist. When cooking a roast or bird with a dry rub, allow the meat to cook long enough for the rub to become dry again, so it adheres to the meat, before beginning to baste.

WEBER'S GUIDELINES FOR GREAT RESULTS

No one knows grilling better than the folks at Weber. For as long as they've been making top-quality grills, they have fielded questions from people needing grilling advice. The following is a list of their 10 best time-tested recommendations, courtesy of Weber's *Real Grilling* cookbook by Jamie Purviance.

❶ LIGHTER FLUID: NO WAY!

There is no reason to use lighter fluid anymore. It's a petroleum product, and who wants that and its foul chemical fumes under their food? Chimney starters and paraffin cubes are much cleaner and much more effective.

❷ PREHEAT THE GRILL

Preheating your grill with the lid closed for 10 to 15 minutes prepares the cooking grate. With all the coals glowing red, or all the gas burners on high, the temperature under the lid should reach 500°F. The heat loosens any bits and pieces of food hanging onto the grate, making it easy to brush them off. A hot grate is also crucial for searing food properly.

❸ KEEP IT CLEAN

When bits of food have stuck to your stainless steel or porcelain-enameled cooking grate, and the grate is hot, clean it with a brass-bristle brush. This step is not only for cleanliness. It also pre-vents your food from sticking. *Note: Use a steel brush if you have a cast-iron cooking grate.*

❹ OIL THE FOOD, NOT THE GRATE

Oil prevents food from sticking. It adds flavor and moisture, too. Lightly brushing or spraying the food with oil works better than brushing the grate. You won't waste oil and you will avoid a potentially dangerous situation.

❺ KNOW WHEN TO BE DIRECT

Direct heat (when the fire is right below the food) is best for relatively small, tender pieces of food that cook in 20 minutes or less. Indirect heat (when the fire is on either side of the food) is best for larger, tougher foods that require more than 20 minutes of cooking.

❻ KEEP THE AIR FLOWING

A charcoal fire needs air. The lid should be closed as much as possible, but keep the vents on the lid and below the charcoal grate open. Remove the ashes on the bottom of the grill regularly to prevent them from blocking the vents. A gas fire needs air, too, which it gets from openings below the grill.

❼ PUT A LID ON IT

For 4 important reasons, the lid should be closed as much as possible. 1: It keeps the grate hot enough to sear the food. 2: It speeds up the cooking time and prevents the food from drying out. 3: It traps the smokiness that develops when fat and juices vaporize in the grill. 4: It prevents flare-ups by limiting oxygen.

❽ CARAMELIZATION IS KEY

One of the biggest reasons for the popularity of grilled food is its seared taste. To develop this taste for maximum effect, use the right level of heat and resist the temptation to turn food often. Your patience will allow for caramelization, or browning, which creates literally hundreds of flavors and aromas. As a general rule, turn food only once.

❾ TAME THE FLAME

Flare-ups happen, which is good because they sear the surface of what you are grilling. But too many flare-ups can burn your food. If the flames are getting out of control, move the food over indirect heat temporarily, until they die down. Then move the food back. As always, keep the lid down as much as possible.

❿ WATCH THE TIME AND TEMPERATURE

If you are cooking in a cold climate or at high altitude, the cooking times will be longer than most recipes indicate. If the wind is blowing hard, it will lower a gas grill's temperature and raise a charcoal grill's temperature. Grilling is both art and science. Pay attention to each.

recipes

When it's time to fire up the grill in your new outdoor kitchen, try these classic Sunset recipes for grilling meat with marinades and dry rubs.

GRILLED MARINATED MEAT

Marinating the meat in a heavy zip-lock bag is efficient, but you can also use a large bowl or baking dish; turn pieces in marinade to coat, then cover and chill, turning pieces occasionally. If the marinade includes a little oil, sticking during grilling is not usually a problem. However, if the meat is very lean or has no marinade, or if your marinade contains a lot of sugar, brush the food or grill lightly with oil to prevent sticking. If you use cuts of meat that are slightly thinner than 1 inch, check for doneness sooner; if meat is thicker—1¼ to 1½ inches—use medium-hot coals and allow a few more minutes for cooking.

- 1 to 1½ pounds tender beef steak; pork or lamb chops; boned, skinned chicken pieces; or fish fillets or steaks, about 1 inch thick
- ½ to ¾ cup marinade (see recipes below)

❶ Trim and discard excess fat from meat (dripping fat can cause flare-ups). Rinse pieces and pat dry; if necessary, cut into serving-size pieces.

❷ Place meat in a heavy zip-lock bag (1-gal. size; see notes). Seal bag and turn to coat pieces in marinade. Chill, turning occasionally, at least 30 minutes or up to 1 day for meats and poultry, 20 to 30 minutes for fish.

❸ With tongs, lift pieces from bag and lay on a barbecue grill 4 to 6 inches above a single, solid layer of hot coals or high heat on a heated gas grill; close lid on gas barbecue. Discard marinade.

❹ With a wide spatula or tongs, turn pieces over halfway through cooking. (For fish fillets with skin, grill skin side down first; to turn, slip spatula under flesh and flip onto another place on grill. Remove and discard skin.) Cook beef or lamb until done to your liking (cut to test), 8 to 10 minutes total for medium-rare; pork and chicken until no longer pink in center of thickest part (cut to test), 9 to 12 minutes total; or fish until barely opaque but still moist-looking in center of thickest part (cut to test), 9 to 12 minutes total. Transfer meat to a board or platter and let rest 2 to 3 minutes before serving.

YIELD: *Makes 4 to 6 servings*

LEMON-PEPPER MARINADE

This zesty, versatile marinade works well on all kinds of meats but is especially good on fish and poultry. The recipe can be multiplied for larger batches; cover and chill up to 1 week.

- 1 teaspoon grated lemon peel
- ¼ cup lemon juice
- 2 tablespoons white wine vinegar
- 2 tablespoons Asian fish sauce (nuoc mam or nam pla) or soy sauce
- 2 tablespoons minced green onion
- 1 tablespoon sugar
- 1 tablespoon olive oil
- 1 teaspoon minced garlic
- ½ teaspoon coarse-ground pepper

In a container, mix lemon peel, lemon juice, vinegar, fish sauce, green onion, sugar, olive oil, garlic, and pepper.

YIELD: *Makes about ½ cup, enough for 1 to 1½ pounds meat, poultry, or fish*

ORANGE-ACHIOTE MARINADE

Achiote paste is sold in reddish orange blocks in Latino markets; if it's unavailable, use 1 more tablespoon paprika (1 tablespoon and 2 teaspoons total). The recipe for this marinade can be doubled. It's also delicious on pork. You can make the marinade up to 2 days before using; cover and chill.

- ⅓ cup orange juice
- 1 tablespoon salted red achiote paste (see notes)
- 1 tablespoon soy sauce
- 2 teaspoons paprika
- 1 teaspoon instant chicken bouillon
- 1 teaspoon minced garlic
- ¼ teaspoon pepper

In a bowl, mix orange juice, achiote paste, soy sauce, paprika, bouillon, garlic, and pepper.

YIELD: *Makes about ⅓ cup, enough to marinate 1 to 2 pounds meat*

HERB SPICE RUB

- ⅓ cup paprika
- 2 teaspoons garlic powder
- 2 teaspoons onion powder
- 1½ teaspoons salt
- 1 teaspoon dry mustard
- 1 teaspoon ground coriander
- 1 teaspoon ground or rubbed sage
- 1 teaspoon dried marjoram
- 1 teaspoon dried thyme
- 1 teaspoon pepper

In a bowl, mix paprika, garlic powder, onion powder, salt, dry mustard, ground coriander, ground or rubbed sage, dried marjoram, dried thyme, and pepper.

YIELD: *Makes about ½ cup.*

resource guide

GRILLS AND GRILL ACCESSORIES

Barbeques Galore
www.bbqgalore.com

Dacor
ww2.dacor.com
800-793-0093

Fire Magic Gas Grills
www.rhpeterson.com

The Iron Works
www.topgrill.com
800-811-9890

Lynx Professional Grills
www.lynxgrills.com
888-289-5969

Viking
www.vikingrange.com
888-VIKING1

Vintage Grills
www.vintage-grills.com
800-998-8966

Weber-Stephen Products Co.
www.weber.com
200 East Daniels Road
Palatine, IL 60067
800-446-1071

PIZZA OVENS, FIREPLACES, AND CHURRASCO KITS

Fogazzo Wood Fired Ovens and BBQs
www.fogazzo.com
626-799-8110

PIZZA OVENS

Mugnaini
www.mugnaini.com
888-887-7206

SMOKERS

Big Green Egg
www.biggreenegg.com
404-321-4658

OUTDOOR REFRIGERATORS

Marvel Refrigerators
www.marvelscientific.com

PROPANE PRODUCTS, GRILLS, AND OUTDOOR HEATERS

Blue Rhino
www.bluerhino.com
800-258-7466

TILE

Daltile
1-800-933-TILE
www.daltileproducts.com

Fireclay Tile
www.fireclaytile.com
495 West Julian Street
San Jose, CA 95110
408-275-1182

CONCRETE COUNTERTOPS

Tom Ralston Concrete
www.tomralstonconcrete.com
831-426-0342

OUTDOOR FURNITURE AND HEATERS

Smith & Hawken
www.smithandhawken.com
800-940-1170

OUTDOOR MISTERS

Koolfog
www.koolfog.com
760-321-9203

credits

PHOTOGRAPHY CREDITS

Doug Baldwin: 19 middle; **Bartone:** 23 top; **courtesy of Big Green Egg:** 30 bottom left; **courtesy of Blue Rhino:** 19 bottom; **Brian Vanden Brink:** 11 top, 21 top; **Wayne Cable:** 104 (carpenter's square, tape measure, margin trowel, caulk gun), 105 (snap cutter, laminated grout float, notched trowel); **Rob Cardillo:** 36 top; **James Carrier:** 2–3 middle, 40–41, 57, 154; **courtesy of Dacor:** 30 bottom right; **Sergio de Paula:** 16 all, 17 bottom, 76, 77, 78 all, 79 all, 93, 95 all, 96, 98 all, 99 all, 100 all, 101 all, 106, 107, 108 all; **Laura Dunkin-Hubby:** 104 (drill); **Ken Dunwody:** 8 bottom left; **courtesy of Fire Magic:** 25 middle, 28 left, 29 bottom left, 29 bottom middle, 29 bottom right, 30 middle right, 32 bottom right (griddle); **Roger Foley:** 6 bottom, 7 top, 13 top, 24 top; **Frank Gaglione (styling by Laura Del Fava):** 1, 2 left, 3 right, 19 top, 22, 23 bottom, 24 middle, 25 bottom, 26 bottom, 27 top, 27 bottom, 31 top right, 31 middle right, 32 top right (grill basket), 42, 46, 52, 56, 60 all, 64, 65, 68, 72–73, 80, 86, 102–103; **Frank Gaglione:** 105 (lineman's pliers), 118 bottom, 118 top, 119 all, 120 all, 121 all, 128 all, 129 all; **John Granen:** 9 top left, 10, 20, 26 top, 27 top middle, 34 top left; **Philip Harvey:** 24 bottom, 49, 157; **courtesy of Koolfog:** 35 top right; **davidduncan livingston.com:** 13 bottom, 18 left; **courtesy of Lynx:** 33 bottom right (tank tray); **courtesy of Marvel:** 31 bottom; **E. Andrew McKinney:** 89; **Jerry Pavia:** 17 top, 21 bottom;

Norman A. Plate: 9 right, 83, 84 all; **Lisa Romerein:** 11 bottom, 12, 154 top; **Eric Roth:** 6 top, 8 bottom right, 18 right; **Mark Rutherford:** 105 (propane torch, wire strippers, slip-joint pliers, PVC saw); **Loren Santow:** 110 all, 111 bottom, 111 top; **David Schiff:** 104 (level, mason's trowel, concrete edger, magnesium float, chalk line, mason's corner block), 105 (tester, tubing cutter, rubber mallet, PVC cutters); **courtesy of Smith & Hawken:** 34 top right; **Lynn Steffens:** 58, 59 all; **Thomas J. Story:** 4–5, 14 bottom, 15, 35 top left; **Dan Stultz:** 122 all, 123 all, 127 bottom, 127 middle right, 127 middle left, 136, 137 all, 138 all, 139 all; **Denny and Sue Thorson:** 8 top; **Dave Toht:** 109, 111 middle, 112, 113 all, 114, 115 all, 116 all, 117 all, 124, 125 all, 126 all, 127 top left, 127 top right, 129 top right, 130 all, 131 all, 132 all, 133 all, 134 all, 135 all, 142 all, 143 all, 145 all, 146 all, 147 all, 148, 149 all; **Tom Ralston Concrete:** 27 bottom middle; **E. Spencer Toy:** 154 bottom; **John Trotto:** 7 bottom, 14 top; **courtesy of Viking Grills:** 25 top, 33 top right (hood); **courtesy of Vintage Grills:** 33 bottom left (grill light); **courtesy of Weber-Stephen Products Co.:** 28 right, 30 top right, 32 top left (rotisserie), 32 top middle left (roast and vegetable rack), 32 top middle right (smoker attach), 32 bottom left (beer/poultry roaster), 32 bottom middle (rib rack), 33 top left (thermometer), 33 top middle left (grill cover), 33 top middle right (chimney starter), 33 bottom middle (grill tools)

DESIGNER CREDITS

Abercrombie and Kent Destination Clubs: 7 bottom; **Karen Aitken & Associates:** 3 right, 42, 46; **Arentz Landscape Architects:** 7 top; **Janet Bell, Janet Bell & Associates:** 80, 64–65, 102–103; **The Bob & Melinda Kitchen:** 6 top; **Sergio de Paula, Fogazzo Wood Fired Ovens and BBQs (www.fogazzo.com):** 8 top, 8 bottom left, 16 all, 17 bottom, 76, 93, 96; **Connie Driscoll:** 18 right; **Ken Dunwody:** 8 bottom left; **Elliott, Elliott, Norelius Architecture:** 11 top; **Exteriors Landscape Architecture:** 4–5; **Fine Landscapes, Ltd.:** 6 bottom, 24 top; **Fireclay Tile:** 102–103; **Fire Designs:** 35 top left; **Deanna Glory Landscape Design (www.glory design.com):** 25 bottom; **Frank Glynn, Sweeney Garden:** 17 top; **Bill Harris Architecture:** 8 bottom right; **Irvine's Design Landscape Architects:** 89; **Raymond Jungles Landscape Architect:** 13 top; **Brian Koch, Terra Ferma Landscapes, Builder:** 52; **Pedersen Associates, Landscape Architects (www.pedersen associates.com):** 19 top, 23 top, 68, 86; **Piedmont Designs, LLC:** 36 top; **Tom Ralston Concrete:** 27 bottom middle; **Ransohoff, Blanchfield, Jones Inc. Landscape Architects:** 1, 2 left, 49, 52, 60 top, 72–73; **Bruce Ridell Landscape Architect:** 11 top; **Allison Rose:** 24 bottom, 157; **Carl Steffens and family:** 56; **Sundance Landscaping:** 9 top left, 10, 20, 27 top middle, 34 top left; **Jeffrey Trent:** 9 right; **Greg Trutza:** 19 middle; **Peter Whiteley:** 83; **Nick Williams and Associates:** 12, 26 top

index